COOKING WITH GANAS & ALOHA RECIPES TRIED AND TRUE FROM MY KITCHEN TO YOURS

RUDINA "DINA" PONCE
Home-based "Chef"

Copyright © 2024 Rudina Ponce
All rights reserved.

DEDICATED TO MY SON,

Joe "Poppy" Ponce

May you fly with the angels in heaven.
I will hold you in my heart until
I can one day hold you in my arms
Sunrise 4/1/77 Sunset 3/3/21

Love, Mom

ACKNOWLEDGMENTS

First and foremost, I would like to express my gratitude to my Lord and Savior, Jesus Christ, for bestowing upon me the gift of life and the opportunities to develop my culinary skills, which have enabled me to create this cookbook. As a child, I fondly recall the aromatic flavors that filled our home, courtesy of my mother's culinary prowess. While other children played outside, I was drawn to the kitchen by the tantalizing smells that emanated from it. My mother imparted upon me the cooking skills she inherited from her mother, Adela my grandmother (RIP) who was an exceptional cook in her own right. Born in Zacatecas, Mexico, Adela believed in the virtue of homemade cooking, eschewing canned goods in favor of fresh, handpicked ingredients.

Through the teachings of my mother, Sylvia, and my father, Eddie 'Sonny' Borgonia, I have gained valuable knowledge and skills that I will always cherish. My mother provided a loving and supportive environment, while my father shared his love for cooking and taught me traditional Filipino dishes that have been passed down through generations.

I am grateful for my parents' dedication to teaching me their cooking techniques, enabling me to adapt them into my own creations without sacrificing flavor. My enthusiasm for cooking was evident from childhood, as I eagerly accepted kitchen duties at church camp and school. As an adult, I continued exploring my passion, collaborating with my mother at Carson High School cafeteria. My culinary journey was enriched when I met Joe Ponce, my future husband, who shared my love for food. Together, we have continued to develop our culinary skills for 45 years, pushing each other to new heights in the kitchen.

I possess the ability to accurately depict every herb in the dish and manipulate its flavors to satisfy my partner's palate. This kitchen, which I am grateful for, has been a valuable asset in showcasing my culinary skills, thanks to my mother's wise words: 'The way to a man's heart is through his stomach.' With his unwavering support and assistance in chopping and preparation, I have found true love in the kitchen.

The tables have turned, and I am now the one doing the cooking. My passion for culinary arts has grown, fueled by my Mexican heritage and the term 'Ganas' (desire). My Filipino heritage has also played a significant role, and I have embraced the Hawaiian culture. My father's best friend, Sinako Simi, taught me the Aloha spirit through his ukulele music and little hula dances at the age of 4. I have come to appreciate the richness of both cultures and their culinary traditions.

As a teenager, I became increasingly passionate about the Art of Hula, not solely due to its melodic accompaniment or aesthetic movements, but also because of the profound knowledge and understanding that was instilled in me by my Kumu Sissy Kaio Kumu of Hula Halau O' Lilinoe in Carson California. Food is just as big in the Hawaiian culture as it is in the Mexican culture with many traditional foods.

At the age of 16, I commenced cooking for large gatherings. Subsequently, I established my own catering business, specializing in the preparation of Hawaiian, Filipino, and Mexican cuisines. I take great pleasure in creating recipes extemporaneously and bringing them to fruition. This approach to

COOKING WITH GANAS & ALOHA

cooking embodies the spirit of 'Aloha'. Aloha means Love, Hello, Goodbye. It's never a goodbye but a hui hou Until we meet again.

Individuals' acceptance and decision to partake in meals at a table featuring ono grinds is immaterial to my culinary passion. My late son, Poppy, and sons Jay and Jack, all possess hearty appetites and relish my creations. I have been blessed with three lovely granddaughters: Sierra Ailana, Kylee Kawena, and Jimena Ekena, and I optimistically anticipate that they will eventually discover their culinary passion and revisit this cookbook, recreating the dishes I have prepared for them in the past.

I am grateful for the love and support of my family, friends, and colleagues like Maggie Fierro De Alba and Anna Pena Kerechuk, who have been instrumental in my personal and professional growth. Anna and I have shared a passion for cooking, establishing 'The Chili Queens' and showcasing our Chili Rojo during Christmas time. I appreciate the support and encouragement I have received from numerous individuals in my life and hope that you will find value in my recipes, which have been carefully developed and refined.

Explore my traditional Cuisine recipes "Tried & True" made with " Ganas & Aloha" Crafted with Passion and Love~Dina.

COOKING WITH GANAS & ALOHA

I strive to be a Proverbs 31 Woman just like my mother.

Proverbs 31: 10,11,15,20,25,26,28,29,30,31

10 She is worth far more than rubies.

11 Her husband has full confidence in her

and lacks nothing of value.

15 She gets up while it is still night;

she provides food for her family

and portions for her female servants.

20 She opens her arms to the poor and

extends her hands to the needy.

25 She is clothed with strength and dignity;

and she laughs at the days to come.

26 She speaks with wisdom,

and faithful instruction is on her tongue.

28 Her children arise and call her blessed;

her husband also, and he praises her:

29 "Many women do noble things,

but you surpass them all."

30 Charm is deceptive, and beauty is fleeting;

but a woman who fears the Lord is to be praised.

31 Honor her for all that her hands have done,

and let her works bring her praise at the city gate.

A Chef' prayer:

Lord bless the hands of those who pass in the labor of love, bringing health to the body from the food they prepare.

Let each instrument they use to make their toil an easier task.

Grant them rest from their passion in the kitchen & let their gift of presentation be honored by those who partake in it. Amen

I hope you find joy in my recipes made from my kitchen to yours

Table of Contents

DEDICATED TO MY SON, ... i
ACKNOWLEDGMENTS ii
CHILI DE ARBOL 2
SALSA DE MANGO 4
MY FAMOUS SALSA 6
GUACAMOLE 8
CHILI ROJO (RED CHILI SAUCE) 10
MENUDO 12
POZOLE DE PUERCO CON CHILE ROJO (PORK POZOLE WITH RED CHILE) 14
ENCHILADAS DE POLLO CON CHILE ROJO (RED CHILI CHICKEN ENCHILADAS) 16
DINA'S FRIJOLES ESPECIALES 18
TOSTADAS DE FRIJOLES 20
SOPA DE FIDEO VERMICELLI SOUP 22
PERFECT SPANISH RICE 24
SOUTHWEST CHICKEN TORTILLA SOUP 26
PICADILLO (MEXICAN HASH) 29
FLAUTAS DE REZ 31
CHILI POBLANO RICE 33
SALSA VERDE CON SEMILLAS DE CALABAZA 35
POZOLE DE POLLO CON CHILI VERDE 37
SOPA ROJA DE FRIJOLES COMPUESTOS 39
BEEF CROCKPOT BARBACOA 42
CHILI RELLENO SAUCE 44
CHILI RELLENOS 46
CHARRO BEANS (COWBOY BEANS) 48
ALBONDIGA SOUP (MEATBALL SOUP) 50
TIPS ON MAKING TORTILLAS HARINA (FLOUR TORTILLAS) 52
TORTILLAS DE HARINA (FLOUR TORTILLAS) 53
MY SOUTHWEST EGG ROLLS 55
CHAMPURRADO (HOT CORN & CHOCOLATE DRINK) 57
HAWAIIAN PORK LAULAU 59

COOKING WITH GANAS & ALOHA

BACON FRIED RICE	61
HAWAIIAN SHOYU CHICKEN	63
HAWAIIAN MOCHIKO CHICKEN	65
ALOHA POKE	67
SAMOAN PALUSAMI	69
BBQ HULI HULI CHICKEN	71
HAUPIA (COCONUT PUDDING DESSERT)	73
THE QUEENS CHICKEN SALAD	75
DINA'S SHRIMP & CRAB COCKTAIL	77
SOTANGHON (FILIPINO CHICKEN LONG RICE)	79
MY SECRET TERIYAKI SAUCE	81
HAWAIIAN POTATO MAC SALAD	83
PORK WITH VEGGIE LUMPIA	85
CHICKEN SCALLOPINI	87
ROUX BASIC WHITE SAUCE	90
MY CLAM CHOWDER	92
CHILI BEANS	94
CRANBERRY PISTACHIO BASMATI RICE	96
MY FINEST POTATO SALAD	98
CILANTRO LIME BASMATI RICE	100
JALAPENO HUMMUS	102
INSANE MAC N CHEESE	104
COLORFUL JELLO COOKIES	106
MY BEST OATMEAL RAISIN COOKIES	108
CRUNCHY PEANUT BUTTER COOKIES	110
SNOWBALLS, AKA MEXICAN WEDDING COOKIES	112
PEAR SQUARES	114
COCONUT CHEWY'S	116
COCONUT CLOUDS	118
JAMMY BAR COOKIES	120
DECADENT CHOCOLATE CHIP COOKIES	122
THE BEST OATMEAL CHOCOLATE CHIP COOKIES	124
FUN FUSION COOKIES	126

COOKING WITH GANAS & ALOHA

- CAFETERIA COFFEE CAKE 129
- MY BANANA BREAD 131
- STRAWBERRY SHORTCAKE MUFFINS 133
- PINEAPPLE UPSIDE DOWN CAKE 136
- CARROT CAKE 138
- TEACHERS CAKE 140
- SOCK IT TO ME CAKE 142
- POPCORN BALLS 144
- PEANUT BRITTLE 146
- OLD FASHIONED FUDGE 148
- CINNAMON RED CANDY APPLES 150
- PIE CRUST (NO FAIL) 152
- SOUTHERN SWEET POTATO PIE 154
- PLATING IDEAS 161

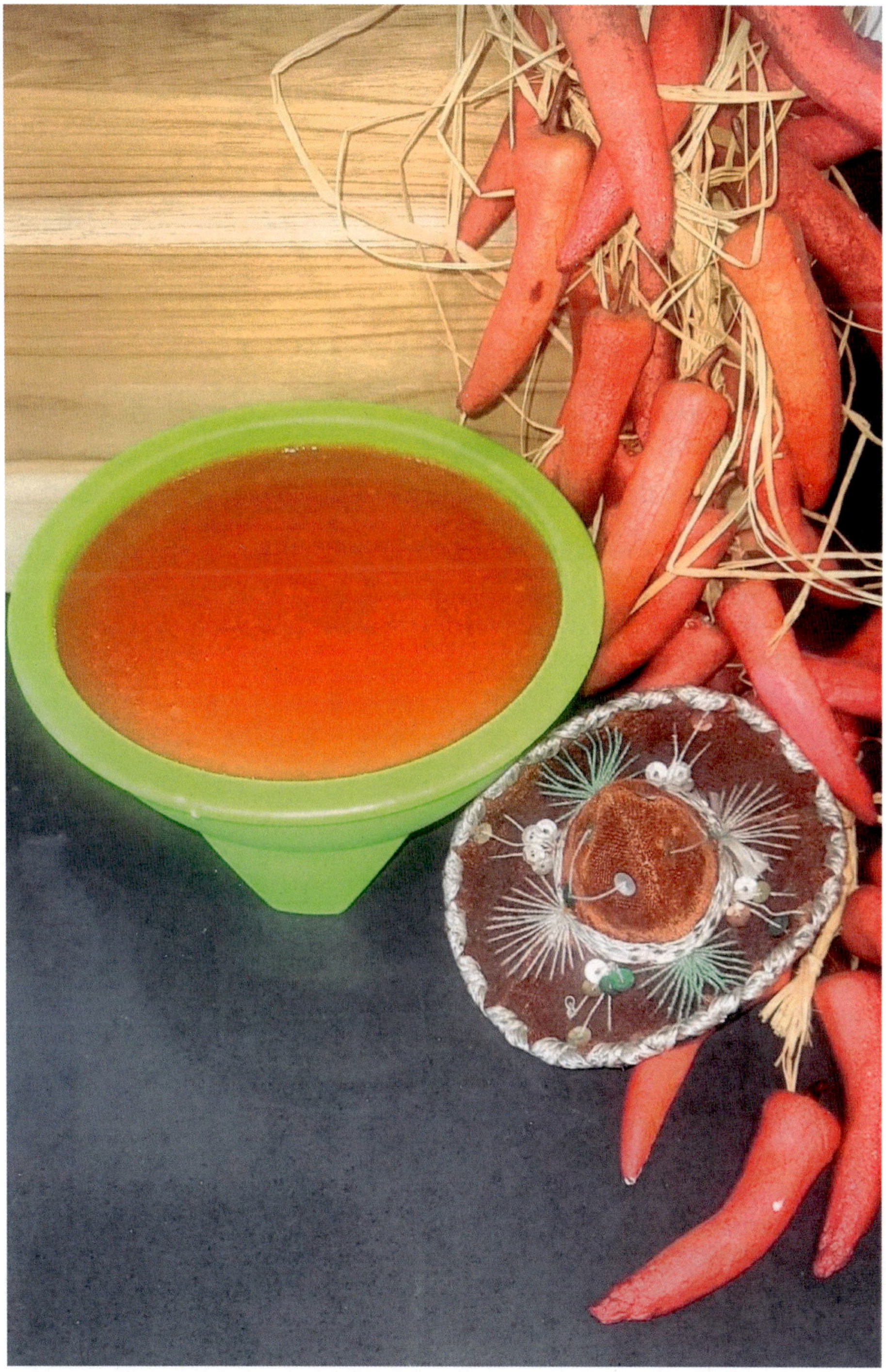

COOKING WITH GANAS & ALOHA

CHILI DE ARBOL

Ingredients:

- 1 8 oz package of Chili arbol peppers

- 1 14.5 oz can tomato sauce

- Salt

- Garlic powder

Directions:

Boil the arbol peppers in a pot with plenty of water to cover the pods. Cook on medium heat, but keep watch as the water boils; the chilies will puff up and the water will overflow. Press the chilies down with a spoon. Cook for a total of 30 minutes. Turn off the flame and place a lid on the chilies. (Do not use a vented lid)

Let the chilies steep for about 1 hour.

Remove the lid and place the chilies and about 1 cup of the chili juice from the pot in a blender. Add 1/2 of the can of tomato sauce, about 1 Tbsp granulated garlic and 2 Tbsp salt and blend on high for 3 minutes. Take a sifter and, pour the blended ingredients into the sifter and sift till all the sauce is out of the sifter. Discard the seeds and skins. Repeat the process till all the chilies are done. Add salt & garlic as needed.

This salsa is super spicy; you can add more tomato sauce to bring the heat down.

This goes well on my Tostadas de frijoles found here in this cookbook.

COOKING WITH GANAS & ALOHA

COOKING WITH GANAS & ALOHA

SALSA DE MANGO

Ingredients:

- 1 1/2 Cups Diced Red bell peppers

- 1 1/2 Cups Diced mango (You can use a can, too)

- 1/3 Cup Cilantro leaves diced fine

- 1 large Purple onion diced

- 2 tsp Granulated garlic

- 1 tsp Salt

- 1 tsp Ground cumin

- 1 tsp Chili powder

- 1 tsp Black pepper

- 1/2 Cup olive oil

- 1/2 Cup Fresh squeezed lime juice (about 4 limes)

- 2 Serrano chilies (stems removed, de-seeded and diced)

Directions:

Place all the ingredients into a bowl and mix thoroughly. Cover and place in the refrigerator for about 1 hour. Drain off some of the juice. You can reserve this juice to put into a blood Mary.

If you want your salsa more spicier, dice a few more peppers.

This goes well with fresh fried tortilla chips.

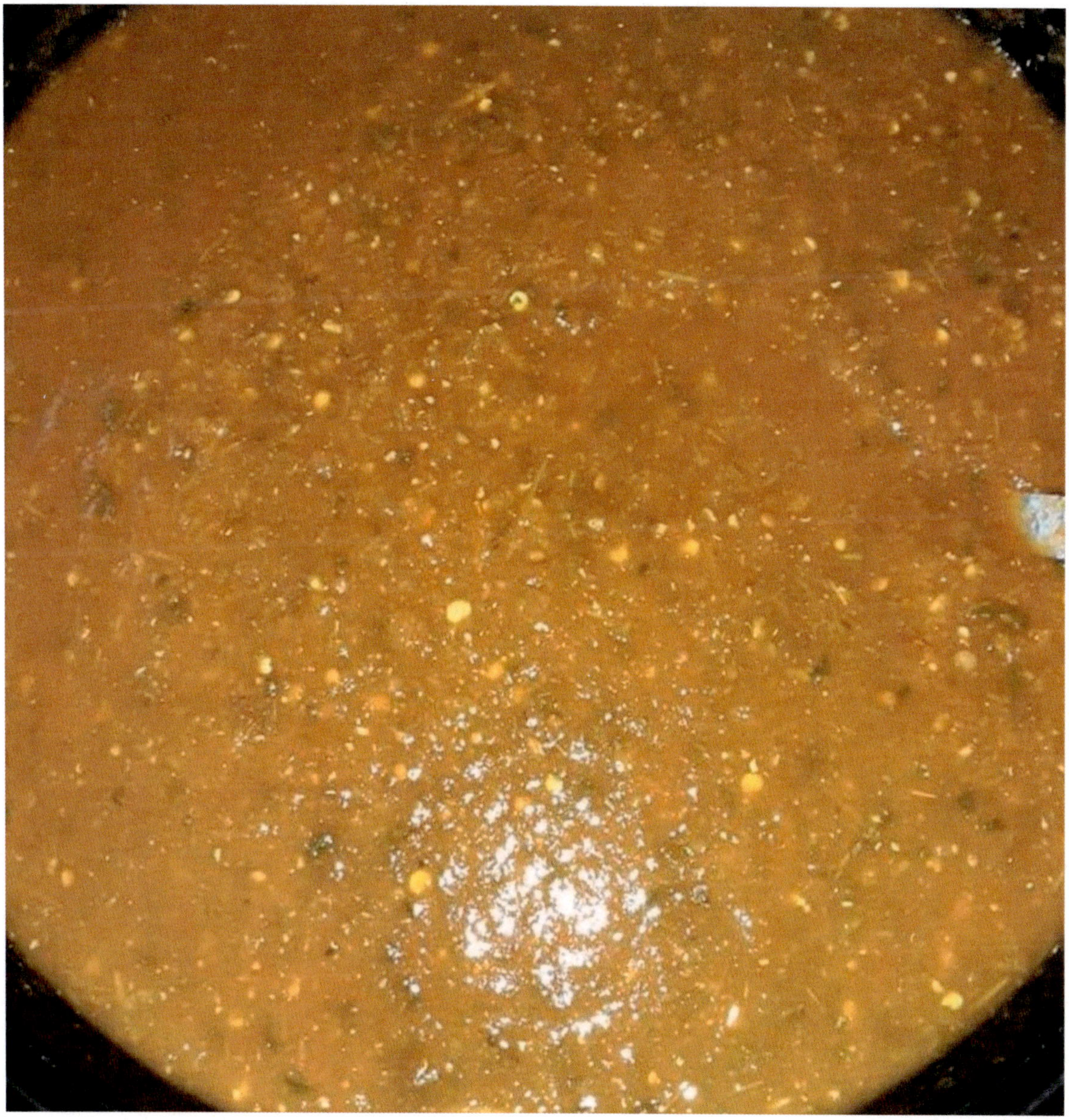

COOKING WITH GANAS & ALOHA

MY FAMOUS SALSA

Ingredients:

- 15 Jalapenos (Stems cut off)

- 1 14.5 oz can Whole tomatoes

- 1 Bunch cilantro

- 1 Medium onion cut into chunks

- 2 Tbsp salt

- 6 Cloves of garlic or 3 tbsp jar of minced garlic

Directions:

Place the jalapenos & onions into a pot with water and boil until the jalapenos turn light green and are soft.

In a blender, add the tomatoes and, twist the tops of the cilantro off the stems and place in the blender. Blend on high until mixed. Pour into a bowl and set aside.

Now take the jalapenos, onions, about 1/2 cup of the juice from the pot, salt and garlic into the blender and blend on high until well mixed.

Add the blender ingredients into the bowl and whisk till well incorporated. Add more salt if needed.

This salsa is a hit at my parties, yet so simple to make. Tastes great with fresh fried tortilla chips. I love eating this while the salsa is still warm.

Place the salsa into a bowl with a lid or a jar. Keep refrigerated.

This salsa has a shelf life of about 2 weeks (That's if you don't eat it all the same day! It's that good)

Note: if you want spicier salsa, you can add a few habanero peppers to the jalapenos in the pot.

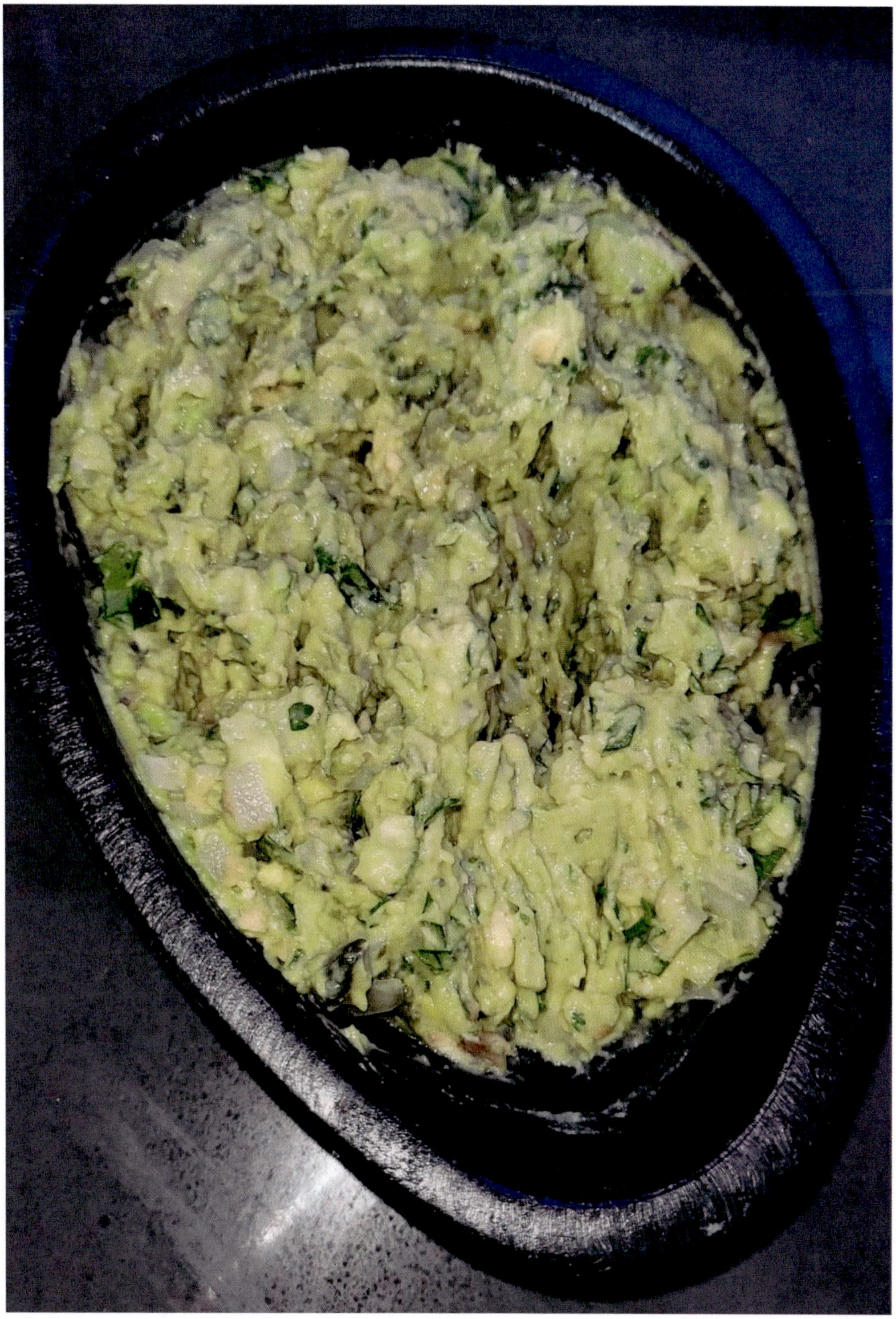

COOKING WITH GANAS & ALOHA

GUACAMOLE

Ingredients:

- 3 Ripened large Avocados

- 1/2 Cup of a chopped mixture of onion & cilantro leaves

- Juice of 2 limes

- 2 Tbsp jalapenos or Serrano chilies (Stems removed, de-seeded and chopped finely)

- Salt & pepper to taste

Directions:

Take a knife and slice the avocado all the way around. Open the avocado and remove the seed by scooping it out with a spoon. Scoop out the meat of the avocado and place it in a bowl. Do the same with the remaining 2 avocados. Take a sharp knife and score the avocados down into chunks. Use the back of a fork and mash the avocados, leaving it a little chunky. Add the onion & cilantro mixture, the juice of the limes and salt & pepper to taste.

Serve with fresh tortilla chips.

You can make this guacamole creamy by using a masher and mash until it's creamy. Tastes great on my Tostadas de frijoles.

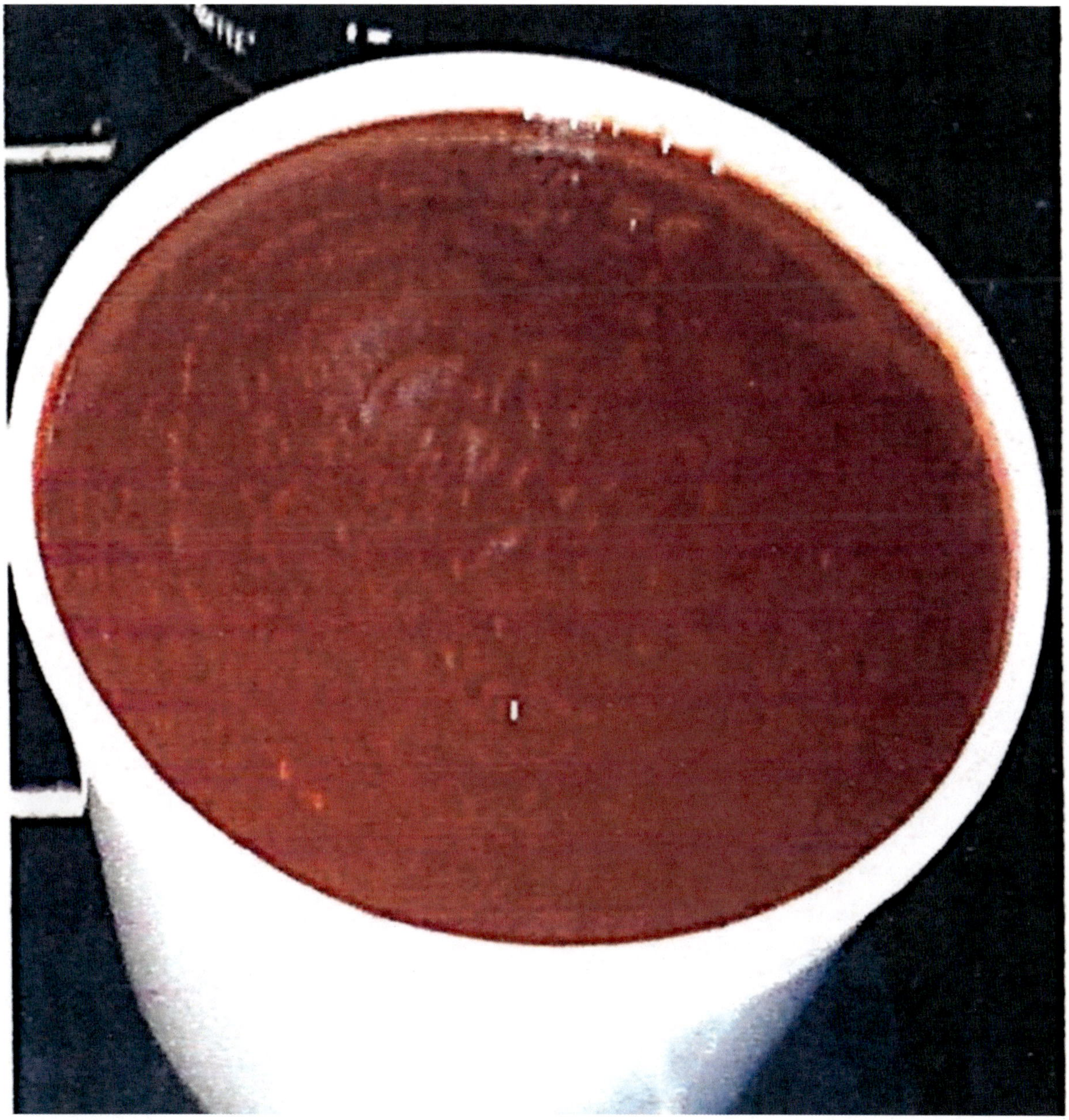

CHILI ROJO (RED CHILI SAUCE)

Ingredients:

- 1 Lb of California dry chile pods (You can use New Mexico pods for spicy)
- 6 to 8 oz of dry Pasilla chile pods
- 4 Garlic cloves
- Salt

Directions:

Cut off stems of chilies, rinse and place in a stock pot with the garlic cloves; put about 3/4 way of chilies. Bring to a boil, but be careful; the chilies will expand and water will boil over. As soon as you see the chilies swell, use a big serving spoon and press the chilies down. When the chilies start to turn color, shut the flame and place a lid on the pot. Let them steep. Remove lid after 30 min and cool down.

Take your blender and, using a ladle, place chilies with some of the juice into the blender. Filling blender 1/2 way, put garlic and salt about 2 Tbsp's and blend on high till well blended. Take a sifter and pour the blended mixture into the sifter over a bowl and crank; the seeds and chili skins will remain in the sifter. Discard and repeat the process till all chilies are blended. You can adjust the texture by using less juice. Chili should be a little on the thicker side, silky. Add more salt or garlic if desired. This is a chili used for Tamales, Enchiladas, Menudo, Pozole, Chilaquilles etc. You can zip lock and freeze in small portions to spice up any meal.

COOKING WITH GANAS & ALOHA

COOKING WITH GANAS & ALOHA

MENUDO

Ingredients:

- 5 lbs beef honeycomb tripe (Found at the butcher counter in your local Mexican store) Cut into 2x2 inch squares

- 6 Pigs feet cut into halves (Found at the butcher counter in your local Mexican store)

- 4 Tbsps granulated garlic

- 1 Onion cut into long chunks

- 1 1.33 oz Package of ground cumin (very important)

- 2 Tbsp Oregano

- 1 #10 (6 lb 12 oz) can white Hominy

- 8 Tbsp Salt & more to taste

- My Chile Rojo (Recipe found in this cookbook)

Directions

Put the Tripe in a big stock pot covered with water and add garlic, cumin, oregano, onion and 8 Tbsp salt into the water. Cook on medium heat covered for about 2 hours.

Then add the pig's feet and cook another 2 hours.

Then add about 8 cups of the Chili Rojo to the pot and the #10 can of hominy. Cook for an additional 2 hours till the hominy is soft. Add more salt if needed.

Ladle the menudo into bowls and top with the garnishes found below.

Serve with hot-fried buttered corn tortillas.

Take a stick of butter and melt in a skillet. Add 1 tortilla at a time & fry till almost crispy yet still pliable.

Garnishes: Diced cilantro & onions, lemon wedges, sprigs of cilantro and use my Chili de arbol found in this cookbook for an added kick of spice.

COOKING WITH GANAS & ALOHA

COOKING WITH GANAS & ALOHA

POZOLE DE PUERCO CON CHILE ROJO (PORK POZOLE WITH RED CHILE)

Ingredients:

- 3 lbs Pork butt bone-in cut into large chunks

- 6 Pieces of neck bones (Found in the butcher section in a local Mexican store)

- 4 Tbsps granulated garlic

- 1 Onion cut into long chunks

- 1 1.33 oz Package of ground cumin (very important)

- 2 Tbsp Oregano

- 1 #10 (6 lb 12 oz) can white Hominy

- 8 Tbsp Salt & more to taste

- My Chile Rojo (Recipe found in this cookbook)

Directions:

Put the Pork butt chunks & neck bones in a big stock pot covered with water.

Add garlic, cumin, oregano, onion and 8 Tbsp salt into the water.

Cook on medium heat for about 5 hours or until the pork is soft.

Remove the meat and leave the bones and juice in the pot. Shred the pork and place it back into the pot with the juice. Add

About 8 cups of the chile rojo to the pot and the #10 can of hominy.

Cook for an additional 2 hours till the hominy is soft. Add more salt if needed.

Ladle the Pozole into bowls and top with the garnishes found below.

Serve with hot-fried buttered corn tortillas.

Take a stick of butter and melt in a skillet. Add 1 tortilla at a time & fry till almost crispy yet still pliable.

Garnishes: Shredded green cabbage, Sliced radishes, Diced cilantro & onion, lemon wedges, sprigs of cilantro and use my Chile de arbol found in this cookbook for an added kick of spice.

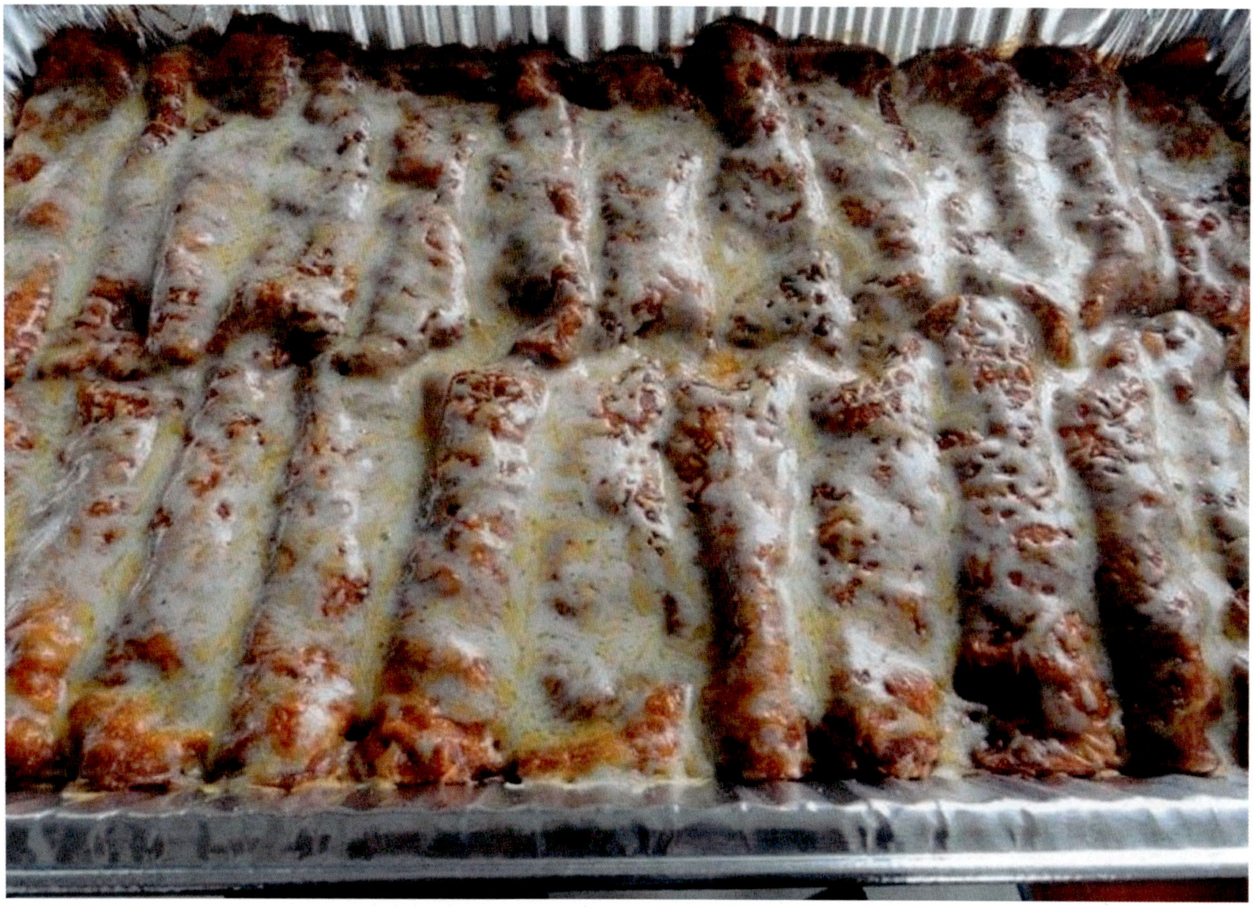

ENCHILADAS DE POLLO CON CHILE ROJO (RED CHILI CHICKEN ENCHILADAS)

Ingredients:

- 1 Dozen corn tortillas

- My Chile Rojo (Recipe found in this cookbook)

- 1 1/2 Cups vegetable oil

- 1 Onion diced

- 3 Chicken breasts seasoned, cooked & shredded

- 2 Cups Cheddar or Monterey jack cheese (A combo of both? Even better)

- 1 More cup of cheese reserved

- 1 Small can of sliced black olives

- 2 Stalk of green onions diced

Directions:

Heat oil in a skillet, place 1 tortilla at a time and fry slightly on both sides.

Place them on top of the other on a paper towel-covered plate. (The heat from each tortilla on top of each other will keep them pliable)

Now, take a cookie sheet or a baking pan and spray lightly with non-stick spray.

Take about 3 Cups of the Chile Rojo and place it in a bowl. Dip 1 fried tortilla in the Rojo till well covered. Place some of the chicken, onion cheese and 4 slices of olives and place at the end of the tortilla closest to you and begin to roll away from you. Place the enchilada flap side down. Repeat the process until all the enchiladas are rolled, placing them next to each other on the cookie sheet or baking pan. Spoon more sauce on top of all the enchiladas till well coated. Top with the reserved cup of cheese and remaining olive slices.

Cover with foil and Bake at 350 degrees for 45 min till hot in the center and the cheese is melted. Garnish with the diced green onions, maybe top with some sour cream and my famous salsa. You can serve my Frijoles specials and Spanish rice. (All 3 recipes are found in this cookbook too)

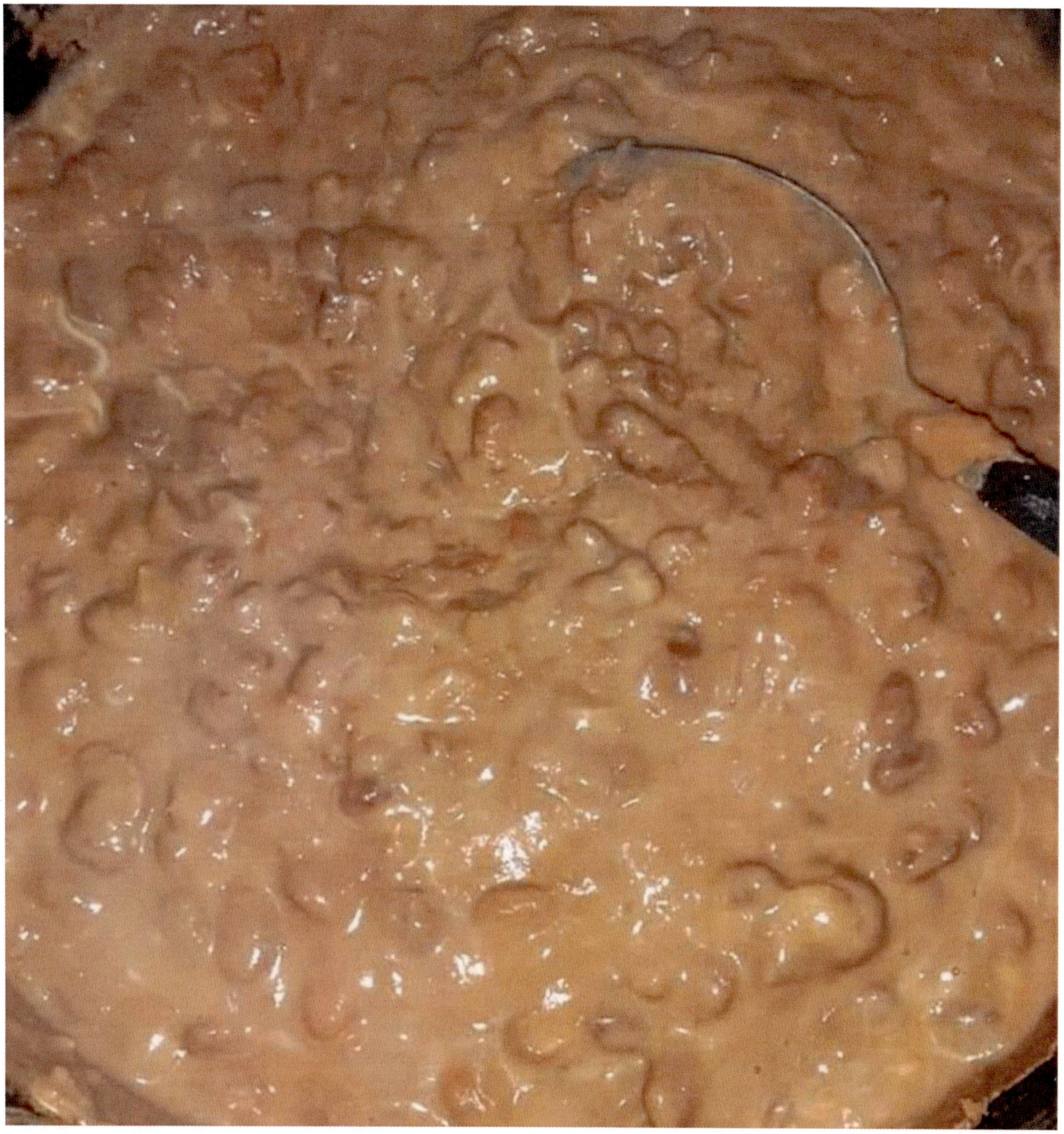

DINA'S FRIJOLES ESPECIALES

Ingredients:

- 2 lbs Pinto beans

- Water to cover the beans, plus 2 more cups

- 1 Tbsp salt

- 1 Tbsp granulated garlic

- 1/2 onion cut in large chunks (For flavor, they will be removed)

- 1 12 oz Can of evaporated milk

- 2 cups shredded Mozzarella cheese

Directions:

Clean out rocks from pintos and rinse thoroughly under cold water in a colander.

(If you don't need the beans until the next day, you can let them sit in water in the pot overnight and it will cut the cooking time in half. They will swell and create a foam of gases released from the beans; skim that off)

If the beans in the pot need more water, then add more to cover them well, about 3 inches above the beans.

Cook on low for about 4 to 5 hours till the beans are soft.

Skim the gassy foam off the beans as they cook.

For soupy beans, you can leave the onions in. If you're mashing the beans, remove the onion.

If you want soupy beans, make sure you have plenty of water; you can add hot water to the beans as they cook.

For these special frijoles, add the water run down till hardly any. At this point, check the salt and I let you know more if needed.

Using a masher, mash the beans and add the evaporated milk a little at a time until you get the desired creamy texture. Add the Mozzarella cheese and continue to mash. (Add salt if needed)

These beans will be creamy and ready to be the side to any Mexican dish. Great for burritos and tostadas too.

COOKING WITH GANAS & ALOHA

COOKING WITH GANAS & ALOHA

TOSTADAS DE FRIJOLES

Ingredients:

- Corn tortillas

- 1 Cup vegetable oil

- 1 head iceberg lettuce

- 1 head Romaine lettuce

- 1/2 Cup finely shredded purple onion (optional)

- 2 lbs shredded Cheese (Jack or cheddar or both)

- 4 Roma tomatoes diced

- 2 Avocados sliced thin

- Sour cream (Optional)

Directions:

Put oil in skillet and heat. Add the corn tortillas 1 at a time till golden brown. Flip the tortilla and do the other side. Place onto paper towels on a plate or pan.

Shred both romaine and, iceberg and cabbage and mix them together in a bowl. (The cabbage adds color, but you can omit it if you wish).

Let's build our tostada...

The best tostadas are used with my Dina's specials frijoles in the cookbook but you can use any mashed beans. Spread the beans evenly onto the tostada shell gently, being careful not to crack the shell. Now add your shredded lettuce and top that with your cheese. Add the diced tomatoes and place the sliced avocados on top. Garnish with sour cream and your favorite salsa.

You can use the avocados to make guacamole instead and place that on top instead of sliced avocados. Place a few sprigs of cilantro on top for added décor. Both my salsas are in this cookbook. The red chili de arbol (spicy) and my famous flavorful salsa.

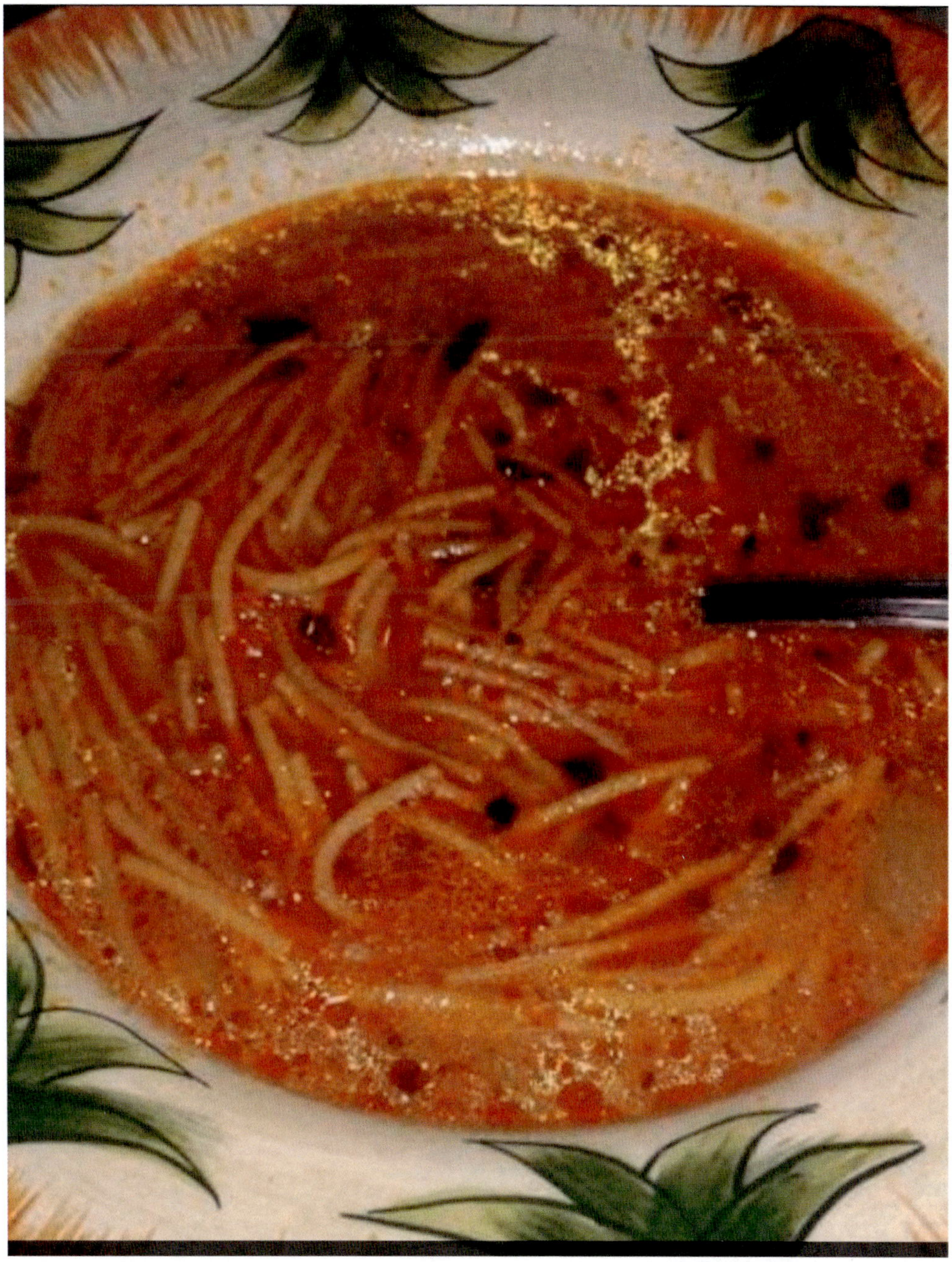

SOPA DE FIDEO VERMICELLI SOUP

Ingredients:

- 2 Tbsp Vegetable oil

- 8 oz Vermicelli pasta loose (If using coiled, then break up the coils with your hands)

- 1/2 Medium onion chopped

- 1 Tbsp granulated garlic

- 1 14.5 oz Can Whole tomatoes (use 4 tomatoes pulled apart with your fingers)

- 10 cups Chicken broth

- 1 Tsp Ground cumin

- 1 Tbsp Oregano

- 2 Tbsp Cilantro leaves cut up

- Salt

Directions:

Heat oil in a saucepan or deep skillet, add the vermicelli and stir on medium to low heat frequently (Be careful not to burn the pasta; it browns very fast); as soon as it starts to turn a light gold brown, add the onions and continue to stir until the onions are fragrant and are translucent. Now add the tomato sauce and tomatoes, and stir till well mixed. Now add the broth and the oregano, cumin, garlic and cilantro leaves. Put the flame on medium to low and continue cooking till the pasta is soft and most of the liquid is absorbed but still soupy. If more salt is needed add to taste.

About 30 minutes. Serve in a bowl and garnish with sprigs of cilantro

(You can also add some shredded chicken to add protein to this soup)

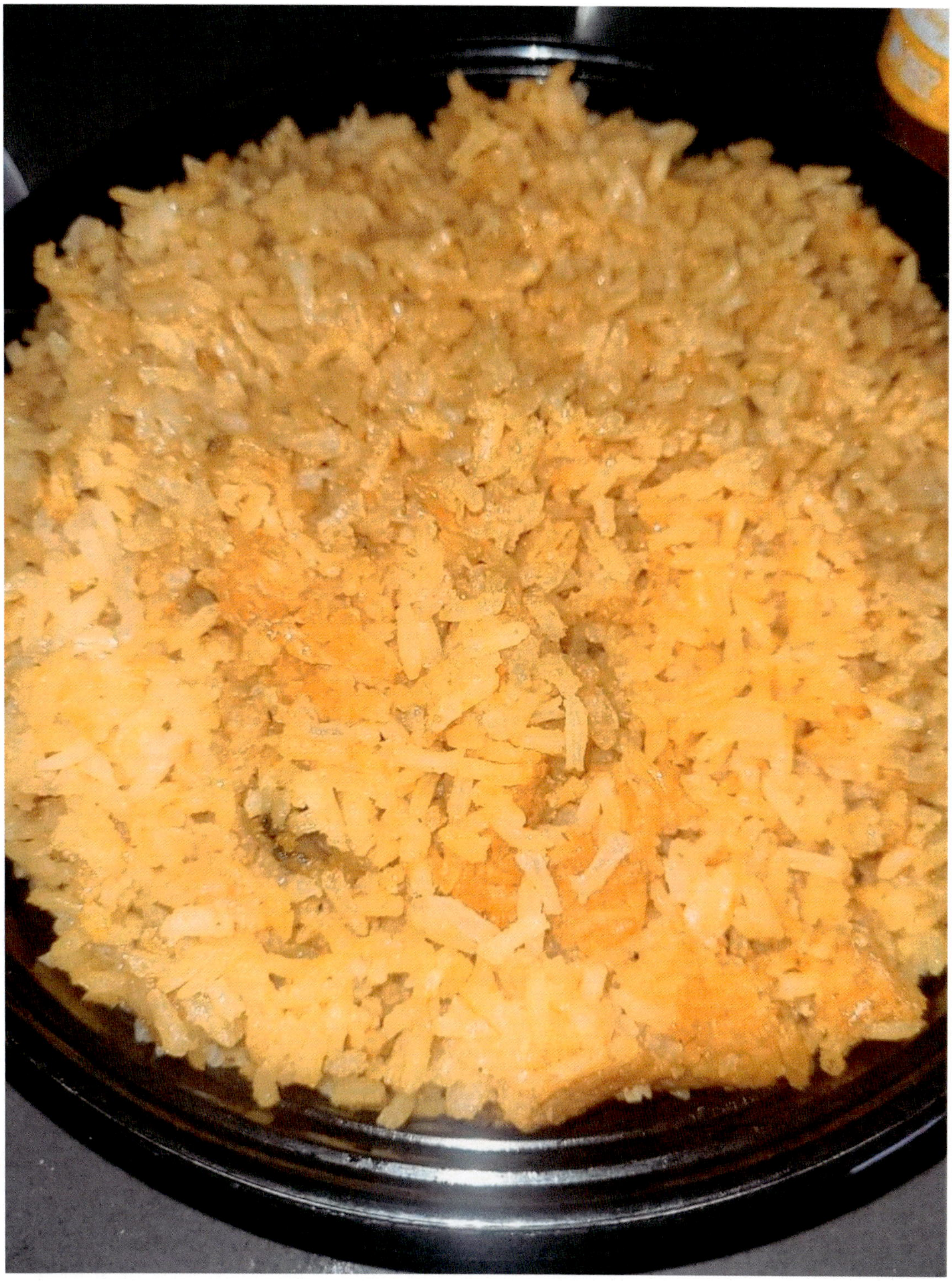

PERFECT SPANISH RICE

Ingredients:

- 5 Tbsp vegetable oil

- 2 Cups long-grain rice

- 1/4 cup onion diced

- 1 8 oz can tomato sauce

- 1 14.5 oz can of whole tomatoes (3 tomatoes from the can)

- 1 to 2 Tbsp Salt

- 1 Tsp granulated garlic

- 1 Tbsp oregano

- 3 Cups water

- (Optional small can 8.5 oz of peas & carrots drained)

Directions:

Heat oil in a skillet or pot that has a tight-fitting lid. (Do Not use a lid with a vent as the heat will escape, causing the rice to not pop) Add the rice and stir on medium heat till lightly browned. Add the onion and continue to stir till the onion is fragrant and translucent; add the tomato sauce and stir well. Add the pulled tomatoes, salt, oregano, and garlic. Stir well. At this point, taste for salt and add more if needed. If you wish to add the peas & carrots, now is the time. Stir well, place the lid on the pot and cook on the lowest flame for 40 min. DO NOT lift the lid while the rice is cooking. After 40 minutes, turn the flame off and DO NOT lift the lid for 15 minutes. After 15 minutes, take a fork and fluff up the rice. Serve.

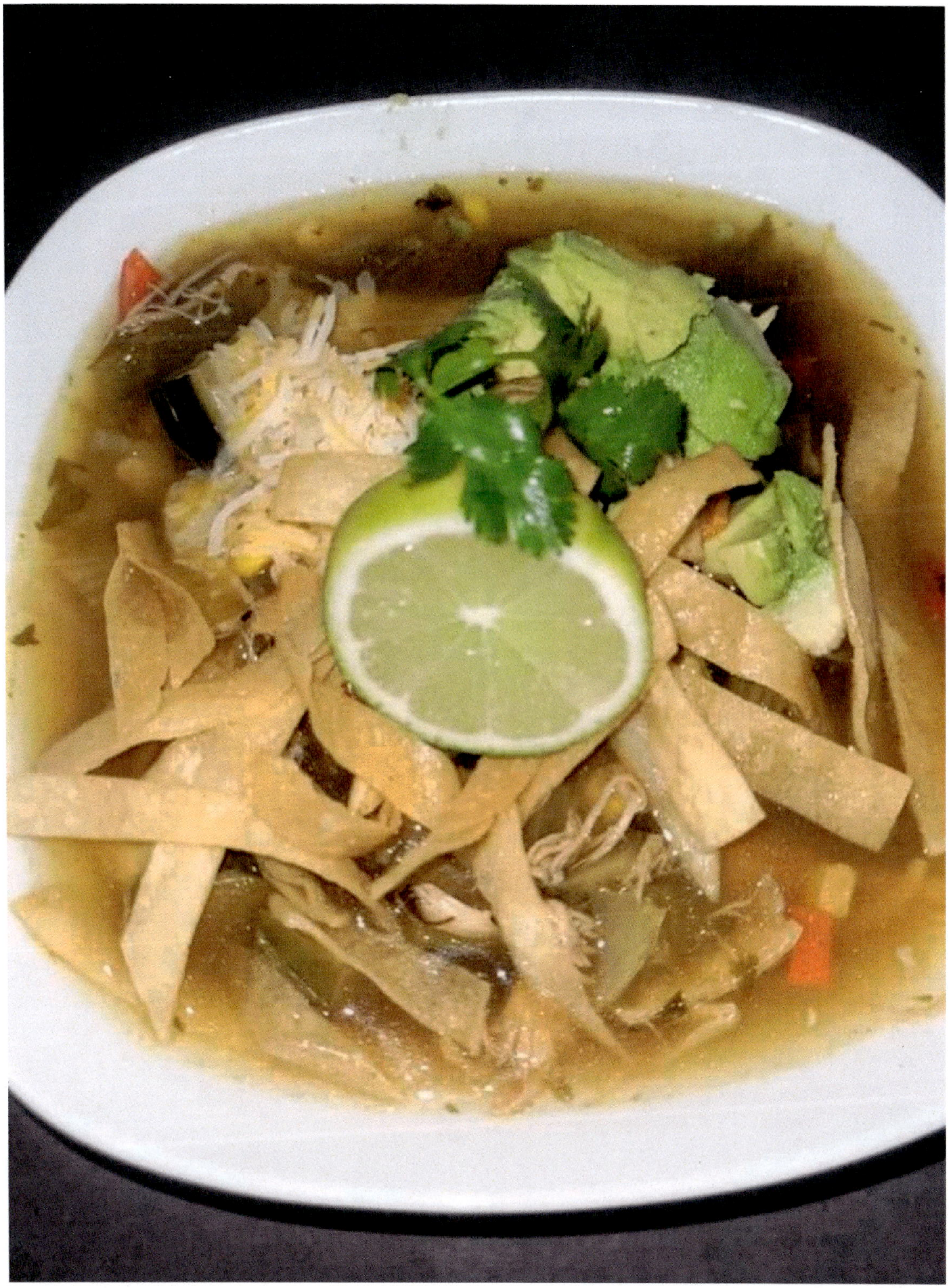

SOUTHWEST CHICKEN TORTILLA SOUP

Ingredients:

- 12 Cups chicken broth
- 3 to 4 Boneless skinless chicken breasts cupped into 1-inch chunks
- 1 Small onion julienned
- 1 Tbsp Granulated garlic
- 1 15 oz Can tomato sauce
- 1 14.5 oz Can whole tomatoes
- 1 15 oz Can whole kernel corn
- 1 15 oz Can black beans (Juice discarded)
- 1 7 oz Can Whole green chilies (Shred into strips by pulling apart with your fingers)
- 2 Zucchinis cut into small chunks
- 1 Bunch cilantro leaves cut
- Toppings:
    - 1 Avocado cut into chunks
    - 1 Cup grated Monterey Jack cheese
    - 4 Corn tortillas cut in half and cut into thin strips
- Salt

Directions:

In a large stock pot, put your cut chicken to boil for about 45 minutes till cooked through. Add the can of tomato sauce and whole tomatoes (pull the tomatoes apart with your fingers until they are shredded into pieces).

Add the corn & black beans and green chilies.

Next, add the onions and the cilantro. Salt to taste. Spoon the soup into a bowl and top with avocado, cheese & tortilla strips. You can add a few sprigs of cilantro stems on top. Squeezing fresh lemon or lime juice and my famous salsa in the soup takes the flavor to another level. (My famous salsa recipe is in this cookbook)

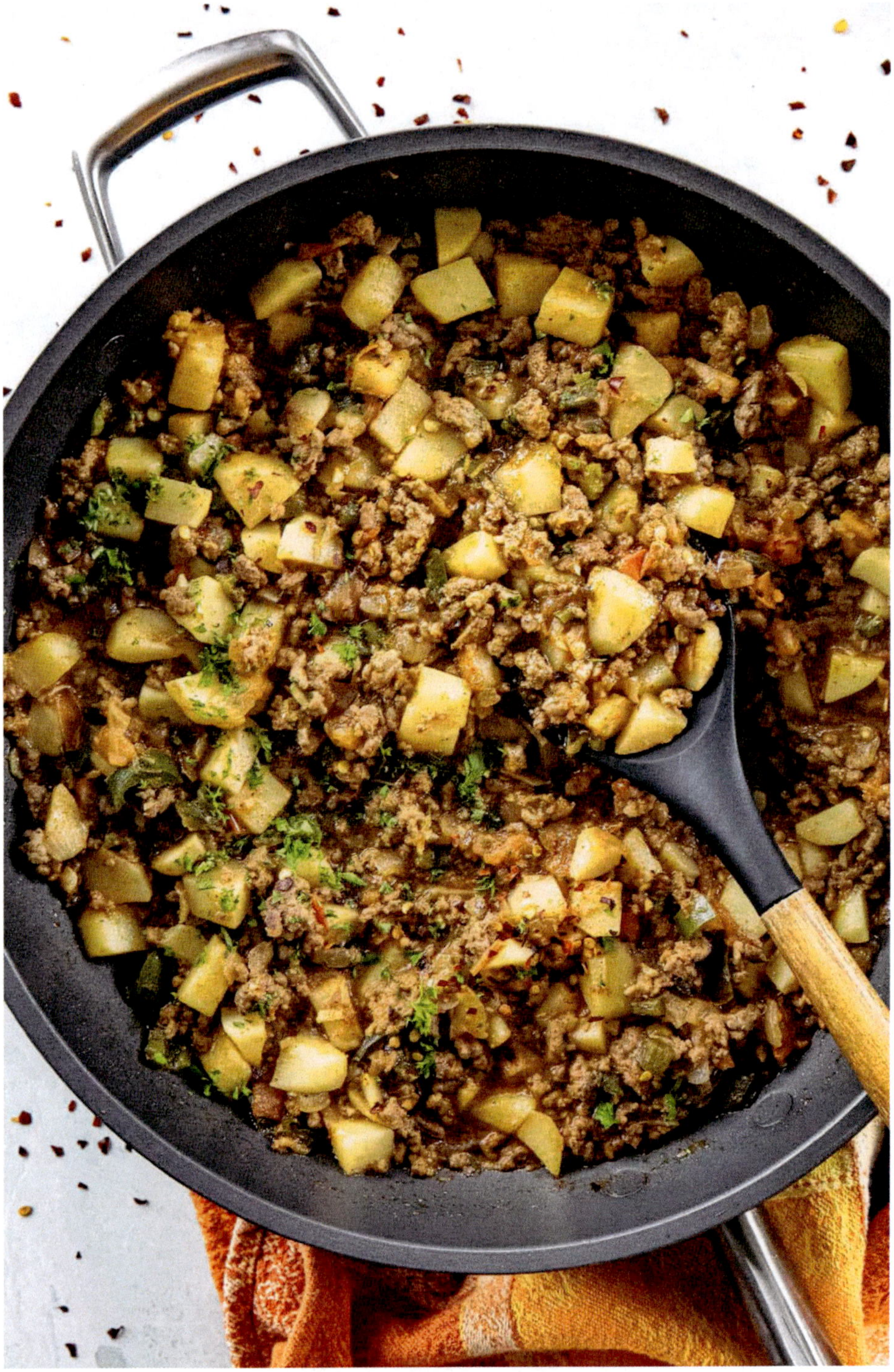

PICADILLO (MEXICAN HASH)

Ingredients:

- 1 1/2 lbs Ground beef
- 1/2 Cup Diced yellow or white onion
- 3 garlic cloves minced
- 1 8 oz can tomato sauce
- 1 14.5 oz can whole tomatoes (reserve juice)
- 1/4 Cup Cilantro leaves
- 1/2 cup chicken broth
- 1 tsp ground cumin
- 1 tsp oregano
- Salt & pepper to taste
- 2 medium potatoes diced
- 2 jalapenos or Serrano's peppers de-seeded and diced

Directions:

In a 10-inch skillet, cook the ground beef, onion, and garlic till the meat is browned and the onions are translucent. Drain off the excess fat. Stir in all the rest of the ingredients except the whole tomatoes. Take 1 tomato at a time and pull with your fingers until the tomatoes shred. Repeat until the tomatoes are incorporated into the skillet. Mix well. Simmer on medium-low for 30 minutes. If you need more juice, you can add the juice from the whole tomatoes. At this point, you can add more salt if needed and add pepper to taste. Cook until the potatoes and chilies are soft. Serve with Frijoles and some Tortillas de harina (Flour tortillas) (Both the Tortilla and Frijoles recipes are in this cookbook)

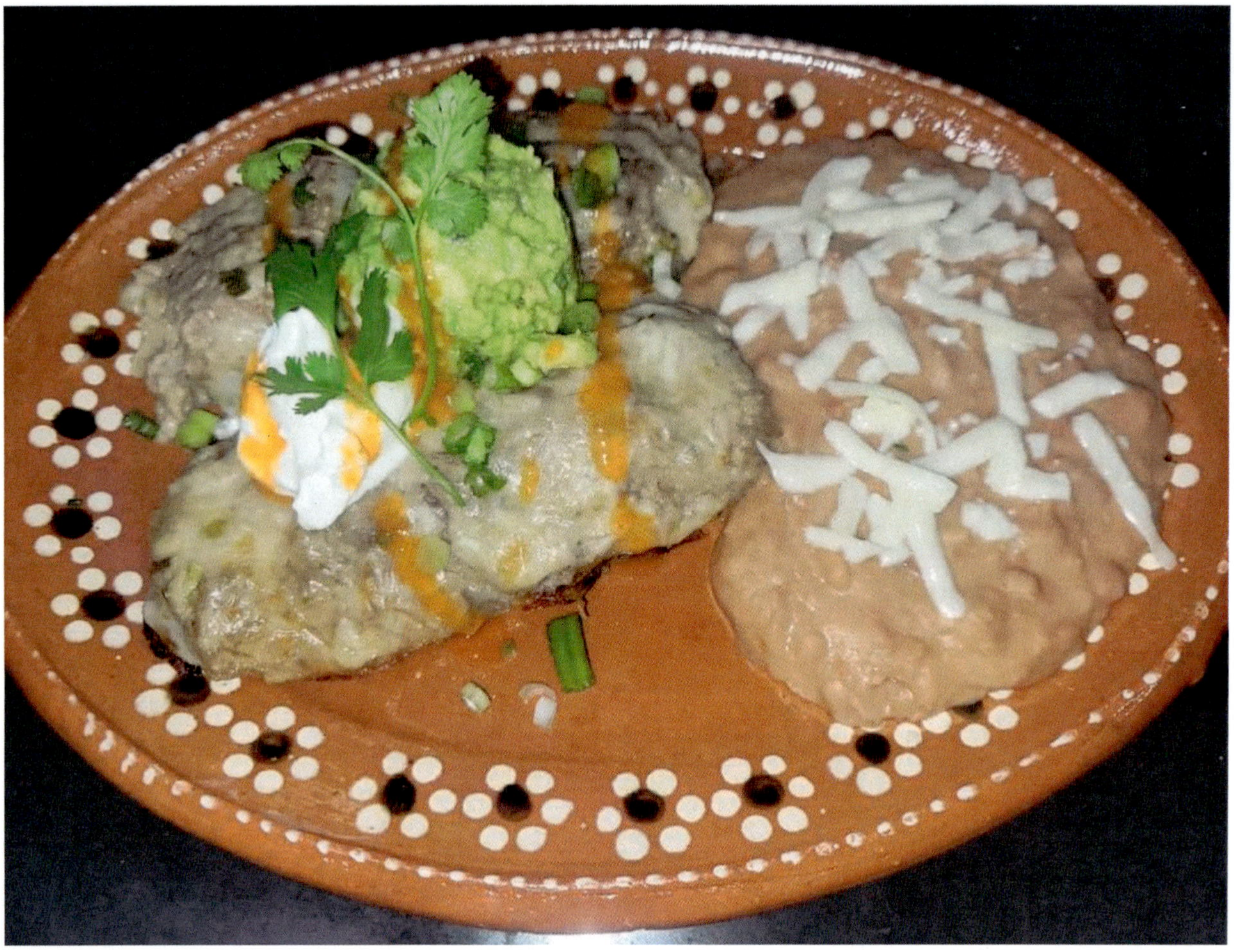

FLAUTAS DE REZ

Ingredients:

- 12 Pack 7" flour tortillas (Not thick)

Filling:

- 4 lbs Beef chuck roast cooked and shredded

- 4 Cups of your favorite canned mild Green salsa

- 4 Cups Shredded Monterey jack cheese

- 1 16 oz Sour cream

- 1 12 oz Guacamole container

- 2 Bunches of green onion chopped (reserve 1/4 cup to the side)

-2 Avocados

(Skin & seed removed & smashed with a fork till creamy; add salt & pepper to taste. Put to the side.)

- 3 Cups Vegetable oil

Directions:

Mix all the above ingredients in a large bowl until well incorporated. Take a frying pan and heat the 3 cups of oil. Place 1 tortilla in the oil and fry until it's light golden brown on each side. Make sure not to fry crispy and still pliable. Lay the drain on a paper towel to catch the excess oil. Continue this with the remaining tortillas, placing one on top of the other. This will keep them hot and pliable. Next, take a cookie sheet and spray it with non-stick spray. Take 1 tortilla and place some of the filling at the end of the tortilla closest to you. Start rolling to the end and place on the cookie sheet flap side down. Continue the process, placing one next to the other. Once all the flautas are on the cookie sheet, spoon the rest of the filling on top of all the flautas till well covered. Take some extra shredded jack cheese and sprinkle it over all the flautas. Place in the oven at 350 degrees for 1 hour. They should be nice & golden. If you need more cook time, do it at 10-minute intervals. Remove them from the oven and, using a spatula, place them on a plate. Garnish with the reserved green onions on top with sour cream and guacamole. You can also put some of my special salsa on top for an extra punch of flavor.

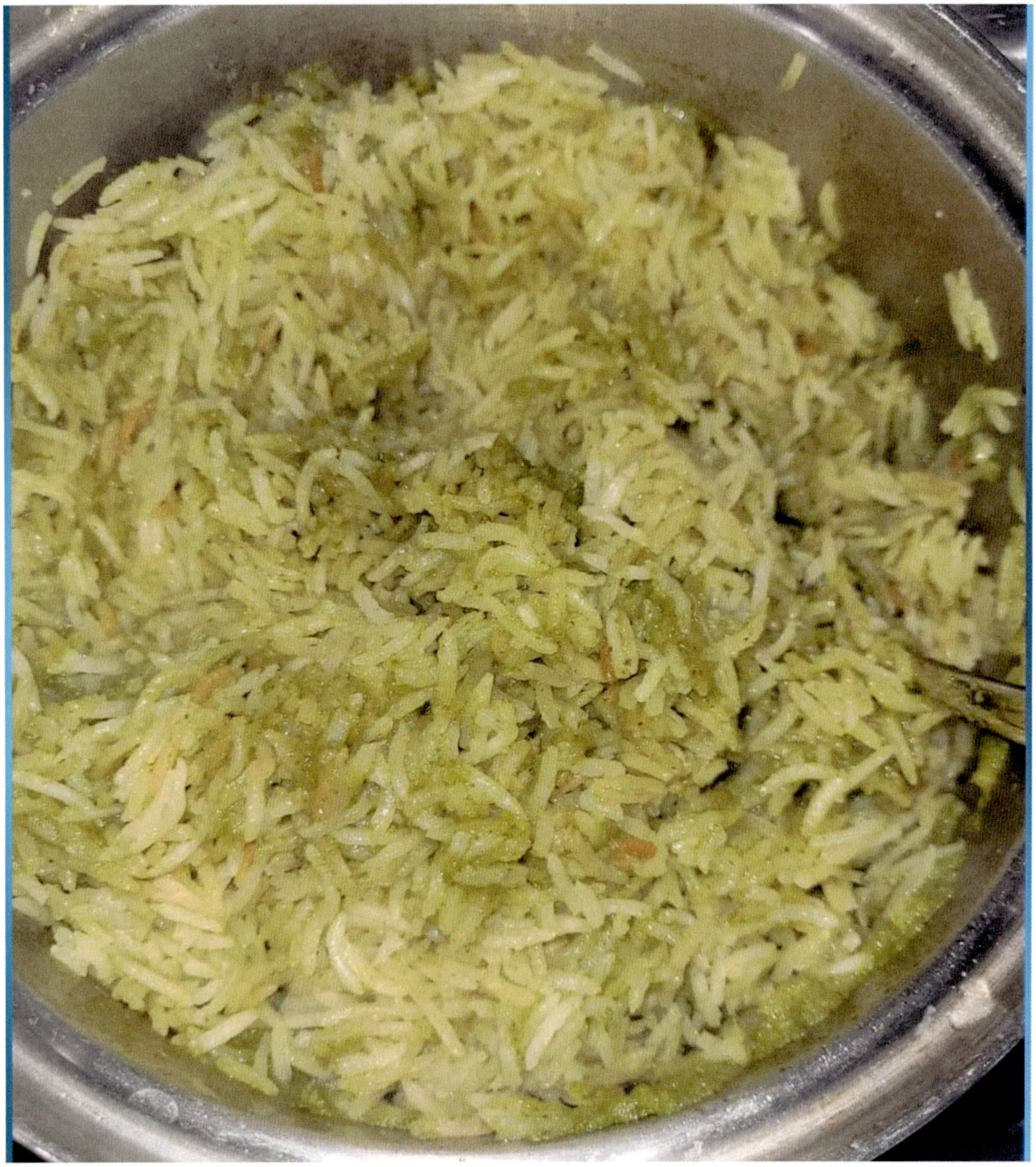

CHILI POBLANO RICE

Ingredients:

- 2 Cups long-grain white rice (Jasmine rice works well too)

- 2 Poblano peppers

- 3 Tbsp oil

- 1/2 large yellow onion (Cut 1/2 of the onion and save it)

- 1/2 Bunch of cilantro tops twisted off the stems

- 3 cups Chicken broth (I like the Mexican Bouillon for my broth)

- 1 tsp Finely chopped garlic

- 2 tsp Dried oregano

- 1/2 tsp Ground cumin

Directions:

Take the 2 poblano peppers and place them right over the direct flame of the burner on your stove. Turning till all the skin is charred. If you do not have a gas stove you can do it in a skillet on the stove. Toast the chilies till the skin gets dark and blistery. Remove from the flame or skillet and place in a ziplock for about 15 minutes. After 15 minutes, remove the chilies from the bag and scrape off all the char. Remove the stem and make a slit in the chilies removing the seeds. Cut into pieces and place in a blender. (Do not blend yet)

Take your chicken broth and pour 1/4 cup into the blender with the cilantro, oregano, onion, cumin, and garlic and blend on high till well mixed. Let it sit. Take a pot with a tight-fitting lid and put in the oil to heat. Add the rice and keep stirring until the rice turns light golden. Add the sauteed chopped onion with the cumin and mix till fragrant and the onion is translucent. Now add the poblano mixture to the rice along with the remaining 2 1/2 cups of broth and mix well. At this point, you can add more salt to taste. When the pot comes to a boil put the flame on the lowest setting and give it one more stir. Let the lid on the pot and let it cook for 35 minutes without lifting the lid during the cooking process. After 35 minutes, lift the lid and fluff with a fork till the rice has puffed up. Serve in a bowl and garnish with cilantro. If you want, you can add some shredded chicken to add protein to this soup. Note Do not use a lid with a vent. No steam can escape; it will prevent the rice from puffing up.

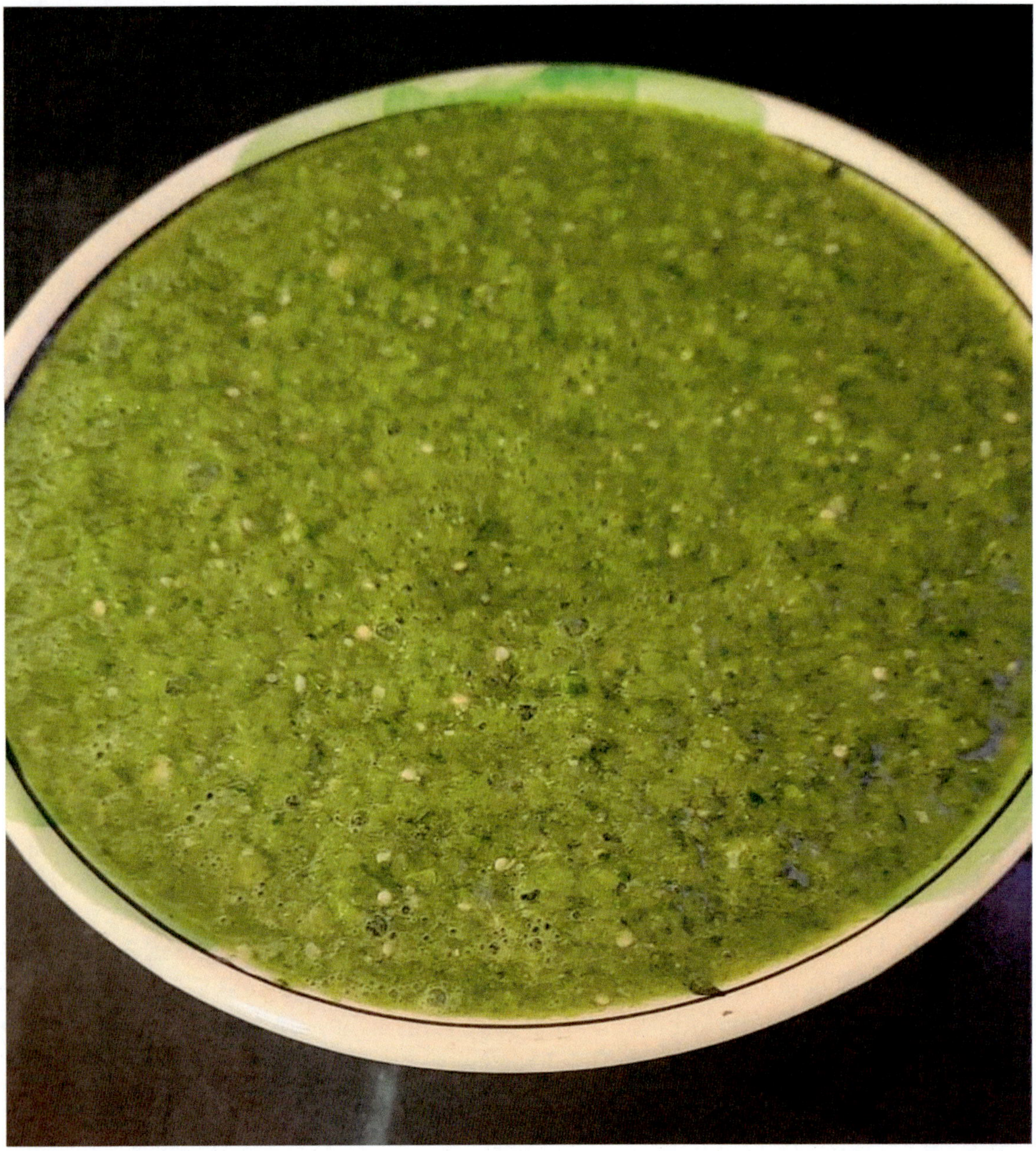

SALSA VERDE CON SEMILLAS DE CALABAZA

Ingredients:

- 5 Tomatillos de-husked, rinsed and cut into quarters

- 2 Serrano chilies cut off stems and slice lengthwise with seeds

- 2 Jalapenos cut off stems and slice lengthwise (you can de-seed for a milder salsa)

- 1/2 Of a large yellow onion cut into chunks

- 4 Whole cloves of garlic skins removed

- 1 Bunch of cilantro tops twisted off with some stems is okay

- 1 Cup Firmly packed spinach (It gives the salsa a deep, pungent green)

- 1 Handful of Pepitas (Pumpkin seeds)

- 1 Cup water (I have used chicken bullion for added flavor, but I omit the kosher salt))

- 2 tsp kosher salt

Directions:

Place all of the ingredients raw into the blender and blend on high. You can adjust the salt or add more chilies if you prefer a spicier salsa. This is so fresh and healthy. No boiling, you don't lose the benefits of the ingredients.

This green salsa is a perfect base for a soup base or Pozole, which you will find the recipe in this cookbook.

COOKING WITH GANAS & ALOHA

POZOLE DE POLLO CON CHILI VERDE

Ingredients:

- 4 lbs Chicken breast

- 4 Tbsps granulated garlic

- 1 Onion cut into long chunks

- 1 1.33 oz Package of ground cumin (very important)

- 2 Tbsp Oregano

- 1 #10 (6 lb 12 oz) can white Hominy

- 8 Tbsp Salt & more to taste

- My Salsa verde con semillas de calabaza (Recipe found in this cookbook)

Directions:

Put the chicken breasts in a big stock pot covered with water.

Add garlic, cumin, oregano, onion and 8 Tbsp salt into the water.

Cook on medium heat for about 3 hours or until the chicken is tender.

Remove the breasts and leave the juice in the pot. Shred the chicken and place it back into the pot with the juice. Add

About 8 cups of the chile verde to the pot and the #10 can of hominy.

Cook for an additional 2 hours till the hominy is soft. Add more salt if needed.

Ladle the Pozole into bowls and top with the garnishes found below.

Serve with hot-fried buttered corn tortillas.

Take a stick of butter and melt in a skillet. Add 1 tortilla at a time & fry till almost crispy yet still pliable.

Garnishes: Shredded green cabbage, Sliced radishes, Diced cilantro & Onions, lemon wedges, sprigs of cilantro and use "My Famous salsa" found in this cookbook for an added kick of spice.

COOKING WITH GANAS & ALOHA

COOKING WITH GANAS & ALOHA

SOPA ROJA DE FRIJOLES COMPUESTOS

Ingredients Part 1:

- 1 1/2 lbs pinto beans
- 1 Tbsp granulated garlic
- 1/4 onion cut chunky
- 2 full sprigs of fresh chipilin (found at your local Mexican Store by the fresh herbs)
- 1 Tbsp Kosher salt

Directions, part 1:

Clean and rinse your pinto beans in a colander with running cold water.

Place the beans in a stock pot and cover with plenty of water.

Add the salt, garlic, onion & chipilin.

Bring to a full boil and, partially cover the pot and cook on low for 5 hours.

You can do the same in a crock pot and cook on high.

Ingredients part 2:

- 7 Roma tomatoes
- 4 cloves of garlic peeled
- 1/2 white onion cut chunky
- 4 Ancho chilies (stems removed, de-seeded & rinsed, cut into chunks)
- 4 Tbsp safflower oil
- 2 Cups of vegetable oil
- 3 Corn tortillas cut in half and then in strips
- 3 Cups chicken broth
- 1 Tbsp cumin

Part 2:

Place the first 4 ingredients into a pot, cover with water, and bring to a boil for about 20 minutes. Cover and turn off the flame. Let it steep for about 20 minutes (do not lift the lid).

While it's cooling down, move on to step 3.

Part 3:

Take the ingredients from the pot with the Roma tomatoes and, place them in the blender with 1 cup of water from the pot and add the cumin. Blend on high until it reaches a salsa consistency. Set aside.

Take a thick, heavy-bottomed pot (such as a Dutch oven) and, place the safflower oil into the pot, and heat it.

Lower the flame and slowly add the salsa from the blender. This method will shock the salsa and bring out all the flavors. Simmer on low to medium heat, stirring occasionally, for about 15 minutes until the salsa is a deep red color.

While the sauce is simmering, take your pintos and spoon them into a clean blender with about 1 cup of the pinto juice and use 1/2 Tbsp of added kosher salt. You can add a little more to the juice if needed (you want a thick, creamy texture). This will probably have to be done in 2 sessions so you don't overload the blender.

Once beans are blended, pour them into the red salsa and stir until well incorporated.

Now add the 2 cups of chicken broth and stir it into the soup until all the beans and bouillon are used up. Simmer for about 20 minutes, occasionally stirring to prevent sticking. At this point, you can adjust the salt.

Ladle into a serving bowl and add the following toppings suggested.

Directions Part 4: Toppings

Use the 2 Cups of vegetable oil and place in a saucepan to act like a deep fryer. Fry the tortilla strips and drain on a paper towel. You can de-seed 2 California chilies, and stems off and cut into squares and fry them (Do not over-fry they burn fast and taste bitter). You can also top it with Pepitas (pumpkin seeds), diced chunky avocado, and crumbled Cotija cheese. You can also drizzle some Mexican Crema and swirl it into the beans with a toothpick. Finish it off with a few fresh sprigs of cilantro.

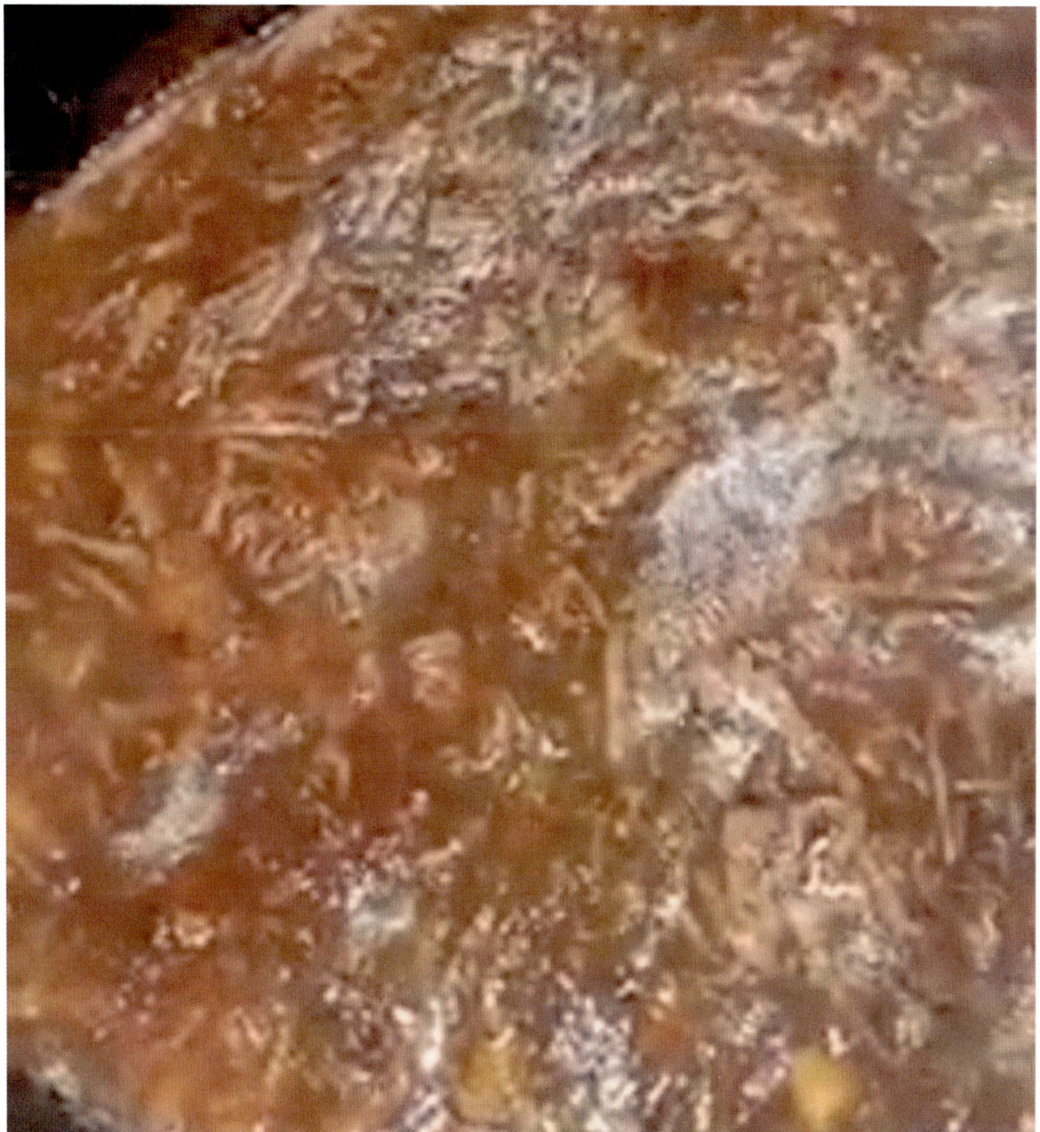

BEEF CROCKPOT BARBACOA

Ingredients:

- 6 lbs Beef shoulder clod roast (cut into chunks)
- 4 1/2 Cups water
- 12 cloves of garlic chopped coarse
- 2 Tbsp each of the following: Oregano, Ground cumin
- 6 bay leaves

Directions:

Place all the ingredients into the crock pot.

Pour in 1 Mexican beer of your choice.

Cook high for 5 hours.

Remove juice, leaving about 1 cup of juice in the crock pot. (reserve the rest of the juice)

With two forks, pull the beef till well shredded.

Place the next 6 ingredients into a blender raw:

- 6 Tomatillos
- 1 Tbsp minced garlic
- 1 Tbsp ground cloves
- 1/2 Cup fresh squeezed lime juice
- 2 1/2 Tbsp Apple cider vinegar
- 2 Tbsp of the chipotle sauce

Blend on high till well mixed (You can add more juice if it's too thick)

Pour the sauce from the blender into the crock pot with the meat and mix well. Cook on high for another 30-45 minutes until it's hot.

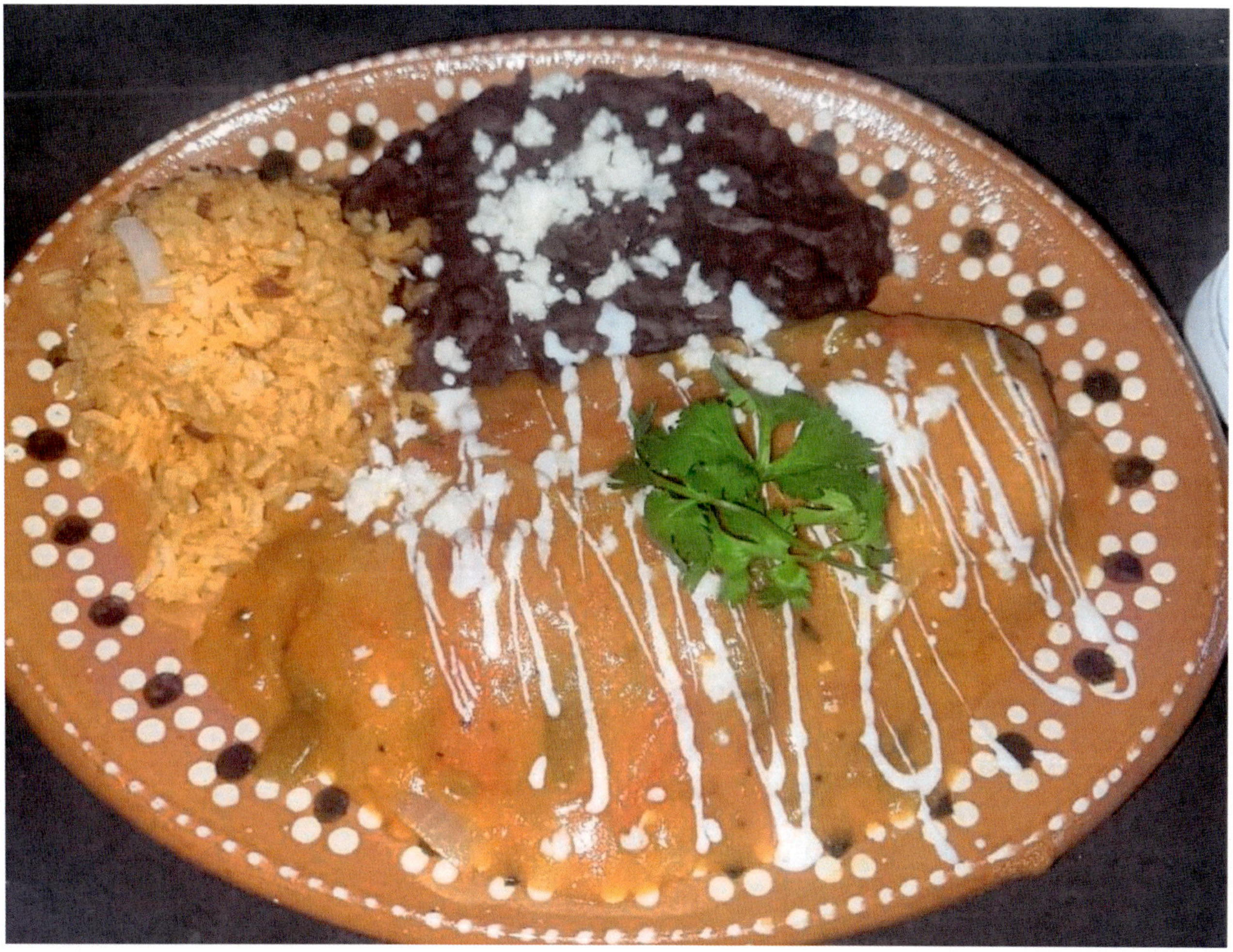

CHILI RELLENO SAUCE

Ingredients:

- 1 1/2 Cup oil

- 1 cup flour

- 2 Cups chicken stock or water

- 1 Small can of tomato sauce or El Pato (spicy tomato sauce)

- 1 Small can of whole tomatoes

- 4 Jalapenos stems off, de-seeded and sliced lengthwise

- 1 Whole onion peeled and julienned

- 1 Tbsp Garlic powder

- Salt to taste

- Black pepper

Directions:

Heat oil in a pan, add the flour using a wire whisk, and whisk till the flour slightly browns; while whisking, add the water or stock slowly till it is all mixed; it should have a gravy consistency; add more water if too thick if not it will thicken as it simmers.

Now add the tomato sauce and whisk; add the whole tomatoes, break them up by hand and pull them apart into pieces, juice and all. Add Garlic powder, salt if needed and pepper to taste. Add the onion and jalapenos and cook till they are softened.

Dip the rellenos into the sauce and, lift them onto the plate and spoon the sauce and mixture over the chili. (You can add habanero hot sauce for a spicier chili).

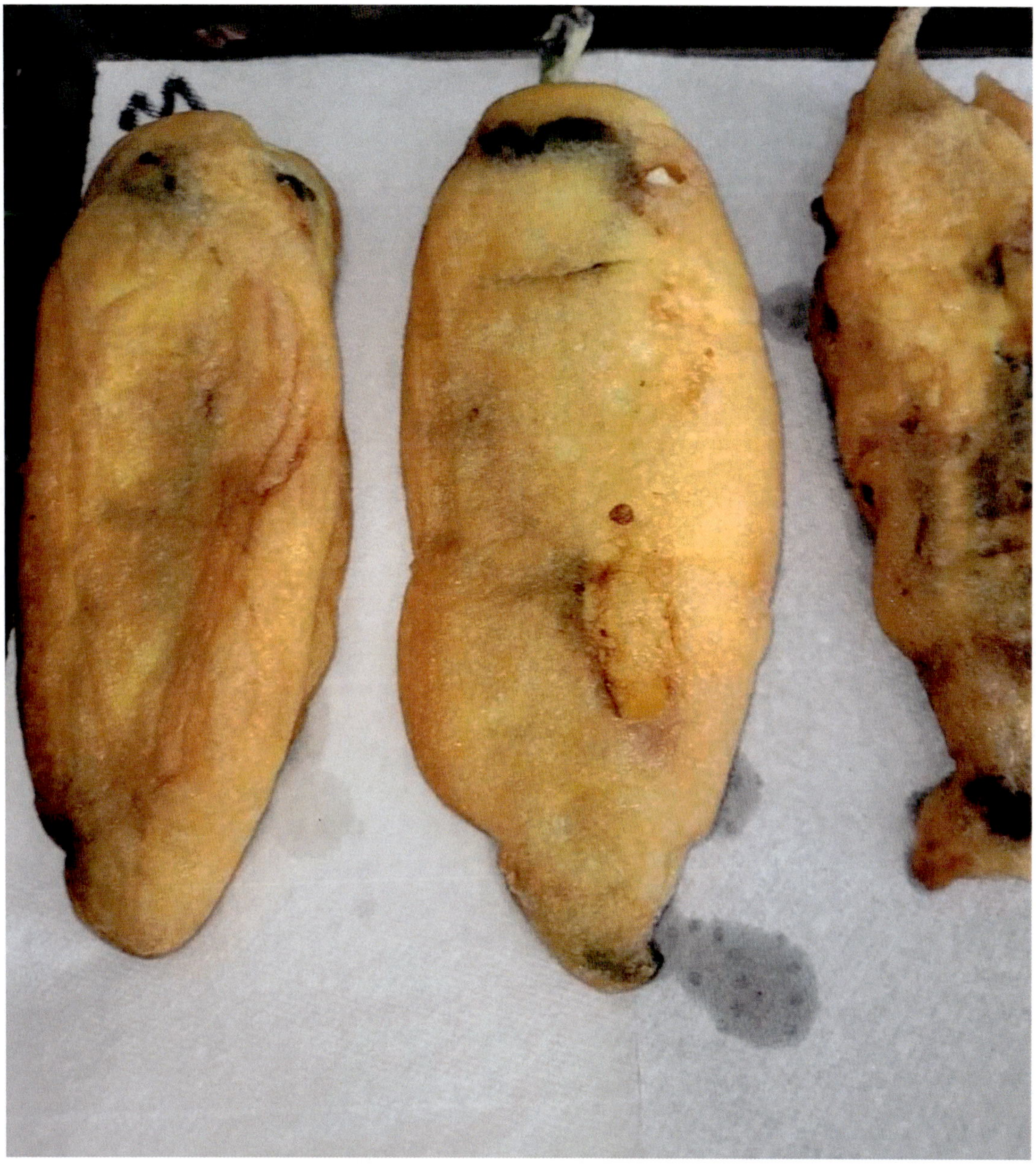

CHILI RELLENOS

Ingredients:

- 3 cups vegetable oil

- 6 Hatch or Anaheim green chilies

- 1 White or brown onion julienned

- 1 lb Jack cheese (Cut into strips)

- About 4 Tbsp Flour

- Salt

- 5 Eggs

Directions:

Place your chilies on a grill or frying pan, pressing down every few minutes till they pop and the skins blacken. Place the chilies in a zip lock for about 20 min. Open the bag and peel the skins off the chilies, place on a plate & open a slit in the center of the chili. Place slivered onion and grated jack cheese in the center. Close them up and sprinkle them with salt & flour so the egg batter will stick. Take your eggs and separate the yolks from the whites. Place yolks aside. Beat the egg whites on high till stiff peaks form and it does not jiggle; then add the egg yolks and beat till mixed; do not overbeat. (Eggs should be fluffy)

Put the oil in a pan and heat on med heat. Carefully dip the chilies into the batter and lay in the hot oil till golden brown, spooning the oil over the top of the batter of chili with your spatula till it is partially cooked, then GENTLY turn the chili to its side and flip (this takes Practice) cook till golden brown. Drain on a paper towel. I also make a sauce that's indescribably delicious on the next page. You won't be disappointed.

COOKING WITH GANAS & ALOHA

CHARRO BEANS (COWBOY BEANS)

Ingredients:

- 1 Pound Pinto beans (cooked)
- 6 Strips of bacon cut into pieces
- 2 Cloves garlic
- 4 Medium Roma tomatoes chopped
- 2 Medium onion chopped
- 1 Large green bell pepper chopped
- 1 Bunch cilantro chopped
- 2 Jalapenos de-seeded and chopped
- 1-12 oz Can any beer
- Salt & Pepper to taste

Directions:

In a non-stick stock pot, fry bacon till almost crispy; add garlic, onion, and tomatoes and sauté till onions are transparent; add the beer and the beans and simmer till the beans are soft. Add the cilantro & jalapenos till the jalapenos are soft. Put in a bowl and garnish with Slices of fresh Jalapeno rings and cilantro sprigs.

Serve with warm corn tortillas.

I usually pre-cook my beans in the crock pot the day before for a quicker meal.

COOKING WITH GANAS & ALOHA

COOKING WITH GANAS & ALOHA

ALBONDIGA SOUP (MEATBALL SOUP)

Ingredients:

- 3 lbs Hamburger or ground turkey
- 5 Large carrots peeled and cut into 1" circles
- 1 Stalk celery cleaned and cut into 1" chunks (Dice the hearts)
- 1 Whole onion julienned
- 3 Ears corn cut into 4's or 1 can corn
- 1 Bunch of cilantro cleaned and cut chunky
- 4 Zucchini washed and cut into 2" circles
- 4 Baking potatoes peeled and cut into halves and quartered
- 1 14 oz Can whole tomatoes
- 1 14 oz Can tomato sauce
- Salt, pepper, oregano, cumin, garlic powder & Chicken bullion to taste

Directions:

Take a large stockpot and fill 1/2 with water; bring to a rapid boil

Season the ground meat with salt, pepper, garlic and cumin

Roll TIGHTLY into balls and drop into the boiling water one by one

Add the tomato sauce, cilantro, and whole tomatoes, crumbling the tomatoes by hand, add the juice too & onion, and season with chicken bullion, garlic and oregano to taste. Let meatballs cook for about 4-5 minutes. Add the celery, celery hearts and carrots, corn & cook another 1/2 hour.

Add the zucchini and cook for 20 min, then add potatoes. It is done when the potatoes are soft. Serve in a bowl with salsa & squeeze lemon. Make a pot of Spanish rice and scoop some into a bowl.

(You will find the recipe for Spanish rice in this cookbook)

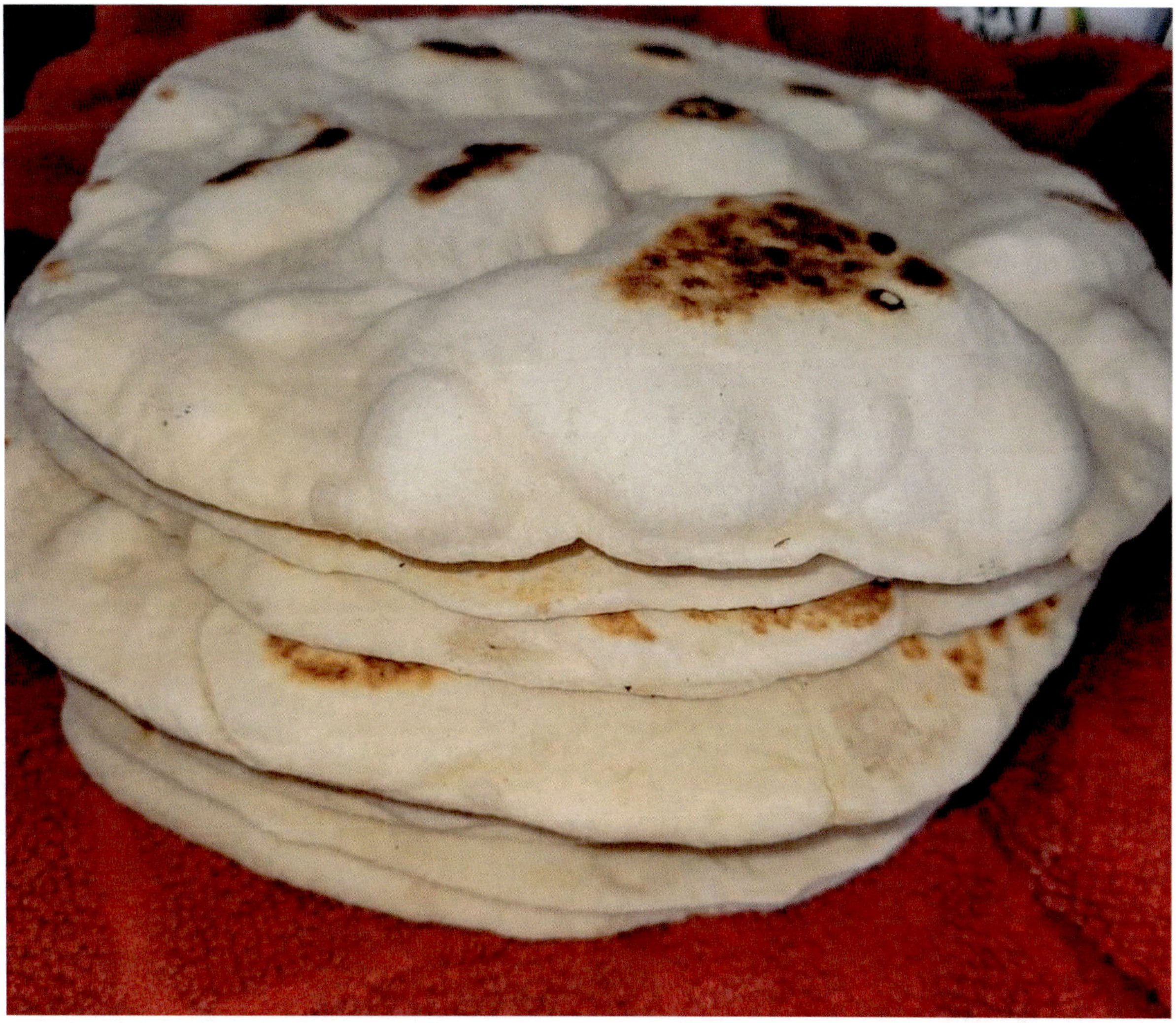

TIPS ON MAKING TORTILLAS HARINA (FLOUR TORTILLAS)

Making flour tortillas may seem easy, but really, when it comes down to it, it's an art. I instruct others, when they ask about making them, to have a soft hand. This recipe starts with flour. I add the salt & baking soda (make sure your baking soda is not outdated) to the flour first, and I whisk it really well. Then, when adding the oil, I drizzle the oil slowly all over the flour mixture with one hand while gently tossing the flour mixture with the other hand until all the oil is gone. Once the oil is in the flour, I "gently" rub the oil and flour between my fingers until there are no clumps. I then add my warm water, but be careful not to use HOT water as it will kill the rising agents in the baking powder and your tortillas won't puff or be soft. I add the water slowly while gently tossing the flour and water together until it forms a dough. Make sure to toss the dough until all the flour is gone from the bowl. Gently turn the dough onto a lightly floured board and knead it gently a few times. Form the dough into a big ball with the ends pulled together downward towards the bowl. Cover and let the dough sleep for at least 2 to 4 hours. Heat your comal (Flat iron skillet) on medium heat and make sure the pan is seasoned well.

Pull apart the dough into golf ball size and roll tightly into a ball. Be sure to keep the dough covered that you're not using so it doesn't get crusty and dry. Place the ball on a floured board and start rolling from the middle back and forth and side to side. As you continue to roll out the dough, make sure you roll from the center and pull towards you and away from you. Turn the dough around repeating the same technique so your tortilla will be round and not like the shape of Texas (haha). Pulling while rolling is very important to get the tortilla bigger. They should be about 6 to 8 inches round. Place the tortilla on the hot skillet and you will start to see big air bubbles peak. This is a good sign you mixed the dough to perfection. Once the tortilla bubbles, leave it on one side for a minute, then gently turn it over to the opposite side continuing to cook another minute to even out the color of the tortilla. If it's not, more time for another minute and place the tortillas in between a dish towel to keep it nice and warm and pliable. You can also place the tortillas in a ziplock or Tupperware to keep them steaming. I hope these tips help you in making the perfect tortilla, continue with recipe is here in this cookbook.

Remember there is no such thing as failure, just lessons towards doing better until you master your talent.

TORTILLAS DE HARINA (FLOUR TORTILLAS)

Ingredients:

- 4 Cups Flour
- 1 1/2 tsp Salt
- 1 Tbsp Baking powder (make sure it's not outdated)
- 3 Tbsp Vegetable oil
- 1 1/2 Cups WARM water (not hot)

Directions:

Mix all dry ingredients in a bowl by hand. Add oil and mix by hand, gently spreading the oil between the fingers. Add water a little at a time, incorporating it all into the flour mixture, and make sure it's not sticky.

Turn the dough onto a floured board and knead for about 3 to 5 minutes. Place back in the bowl and cover with a warm, moist towel for no less than 30 minutes.

Make balls the size of a golf ball.

Roll out circles about 7 inches on a lightly floured board and place on a comal (cast iron flat skillet) on medium heat. Place the tortilla until it bubbles, lift, flip, and press down gently (use a spatula to prevent steam burn). Flip once again and place between damp paper towels tucked into a dish towel to keep warm and pliable. After the third one, place those in a ziplock bag. Makes about 16 7-inch round tortillas.

I like to make the dough the day before, saran wrap it, and roll it the next day; they are easier to roll and softer.

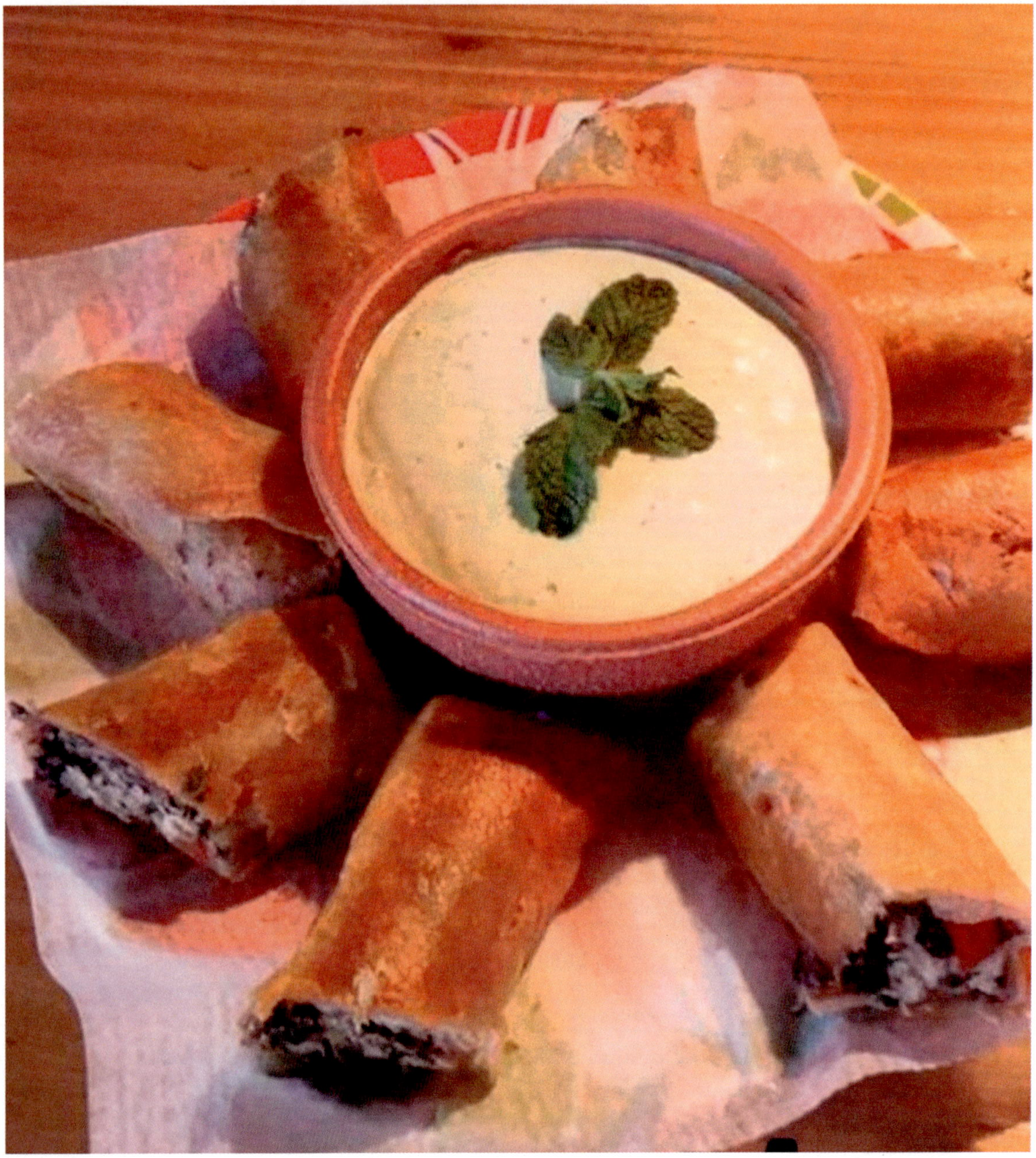

MY SOUTHWEST EGG ROLLS

Ingredients:

- 3 Chicken breasts boiled, seasoned & shredded
- 1 15 oz Can Black beans well drained
- 1 15 oz Can sweet whole kernel corn well drained
- 1 5m can diced jalapenos drained
- 1 Stalk green onion chopped
- 2 Red bell peppers de-seeded and diced
- 1 lb Shredded jack cheese
- 1 Bag of Frozen spinach thawed (All excess water squeezed out)
- 1 Pkg of Small size flour tortillas (Not thick ones)

Directions:

Sauté everything (except the cheese) in a large skillet with a little oil. Season the mixture with 1/2 tsp each of salt, pepper, cayenne, cumin, chili powder, and 2 tbsp of dry or fresh parsley.

Cool completely.

Add the cheese and mix thoroughly.

Spoon the mixture into the tortilla diagonally. Roll over the corner once, fold in the outer sides to the center, and continue to roll tightly to the end. (Makes about a dozen egg rolls depending on how fat you roll).

Fry in hot oil in a frying pan until golden brown (a deep fryer works well). Drain and cool for 5 minutes. Cut in half diagonally and serve warm with dipping sauce.

For the sauce:

Blend 1 avocado, 2 cups ranch dressing, 1/4 cup water, and salt & pepper to taste in a blender. Blend on high until well-mixed and creamy.

COOKING WITH GANAS & ALOHA

CHAMPURRADO (HOT CORN & CHOCOLATE DRINK)

Ingredients:

- 1/4 Cup Fresh masa or (1/2 Cup masa flour mixed with 1/4 Cup hot water)
- 2 1/4 Cup Milk
- 1 1/2 Cups water
- 1 Disk of Mexican chocolate like Abuelita or Ibarra brand
- 3 Tbsp Piloncillo or 1/3 Cup brown sugar plus 2 Tsp molasses
- 1/4 Tsp Crushed aniseed or star anise

Directions:

Put water & masa into a blender & blend till smooth.

Place the masa into a saucepan and add the milk & chocolate & the, piloncillo or (alternate sugar with molasses) add the Aniseed & simmer. Whisk till the chocolate is melted and strain through a sieve. Serve hot. In a Mexican Jarrito mug!

This is my favorite drink during the winter months and this recipe is tried and true.

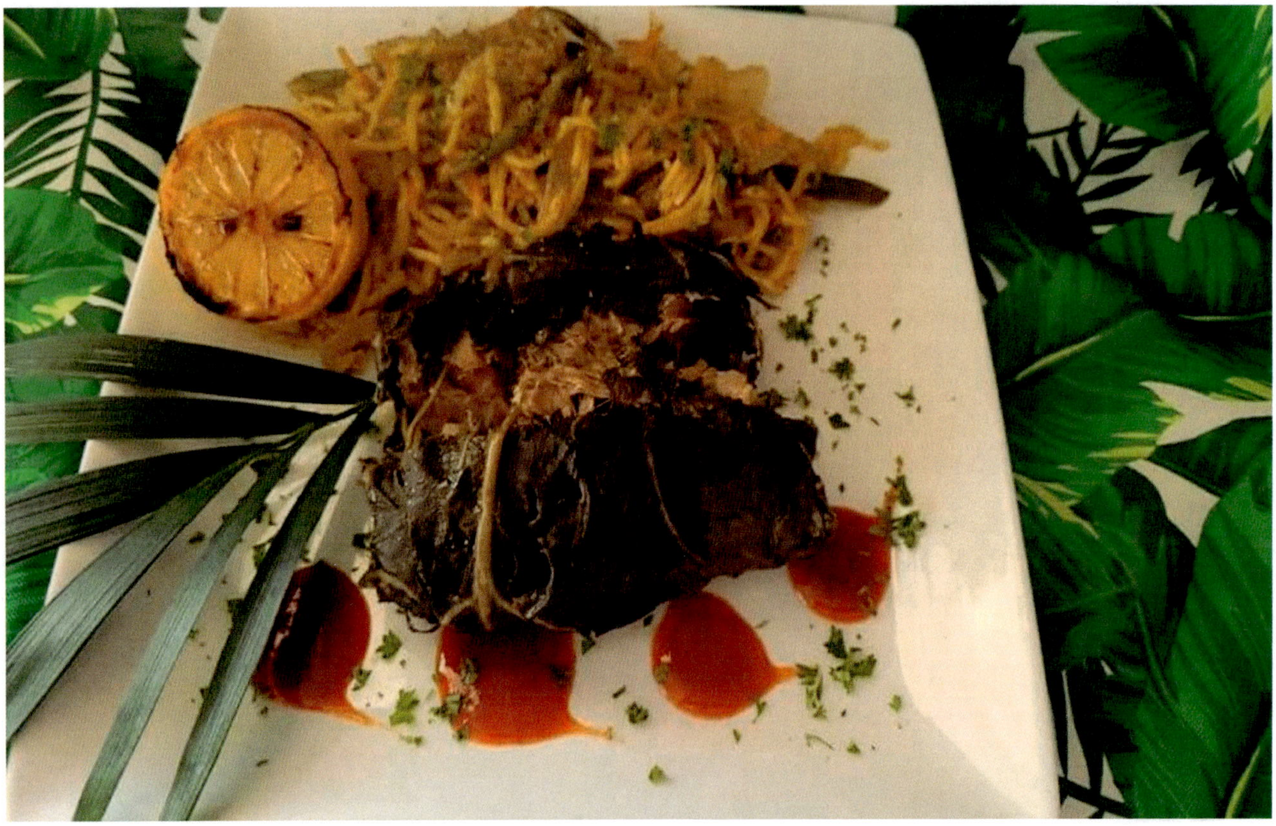

HAWAIIAN PORK LAULAU

Ingredients:

- 8 lbs boneless Pork butt (Cut into 2X2 inch cubes)

- 6 lbs Pork belly cut into 1x1 inch cubes

- Hawaiian coarse sea salt

- Coarse Black pepper

- Aluminum foil sheets (You will use 2 sheets per laulau)

- You can use the roll of foil and cut yourself

- 10 lbs Taro leaves (assorted sizes are good)

- 1 large steam pot

Directions:

Place the 2 cut meats into a huge mixing bowl. Add the salt and pepper and toss to coat evenly. There is no real measurement for the salt just make sure there is plenty to coat the meat. Adjust to your taste. Rinse the leaves and set them aside by size. Take a large taro leaf in the palm of your hand and place a smaller pocket in the pocket of the leaf upside down. Place about 4 pieces of meat and 2 pieces of belly into the center of the pocket of the leaf, roll the bottom of the leaf up towards the center, then pull the sides inwards and continue to roll to the top like a fat burrito. Place the laulau towards the bottom of the foil and roll up, bringing the side in and continue rolling like a burrito. (If using foil sheets, repeat the process again in the second foil, overlapping the first one. Continue till all leaves and meat are used up. Place them in the steam pot, making sure you have water covering about 2 inches higher than the steam plate at the bottom. Layer the laulau and cover with a lid. Cook on high for about 30 minutes then lower to medium flame for 4 1/2 hours. After the flame is turned off and, check the laulau to make sure the meat is tender & return the laulau to the pot and let steep for 1/2 hour before removing it from the pot. Garnish with sriracha and serve with a side of White or fried rice.

COOKING WITH GANAS & ALOHA

BACON FRIED RICE

Ingredients:

- 6 Cups cooked long-grain white rice

- 1 lb Bacon

- 5 Ribs of celery diced

- 1 Bunch green onion chopped

- 2 Raw eggs

- 1 Can peas & carrots

- Granulated garlic

- Coarse black pepper

- Kikkoman soy sauce (I use Swan Soy Sauce, which you can find at your local Filipino or Asian market)

Directions:

Cut bacon into pieces and fry them in a large frying pan till almost crispy. Put the bacon and grease into a bowl to the side with the exception of 1/2 of it, and leave it in the frying pan... Take 1/2 of the celery & green onions and sauté them in the bacon & grease for about 2 min. Add 1/2 of the rice and toss the celery, green onion and rice till mixed; add about 1 Tbsp Granulated garlic and 1 Tsp black pepper; sprinkle the rice with soy sauce till the white of rice doesn't show. Mix well, add 1/2 can of peas & carrots mix again. Push the rice to the back of the pan and crack 1 egg in a little oil in the space and scramble with the spoon or spatula till egg is scrambled & cooked. Incorporate it into the rice mixture. Place in a bowl or pan and cover. Repeat the process with 2nd half. Adjust the garlic & pepper to taste. If you triple this recipe, it yields 1 full foil catering pan.

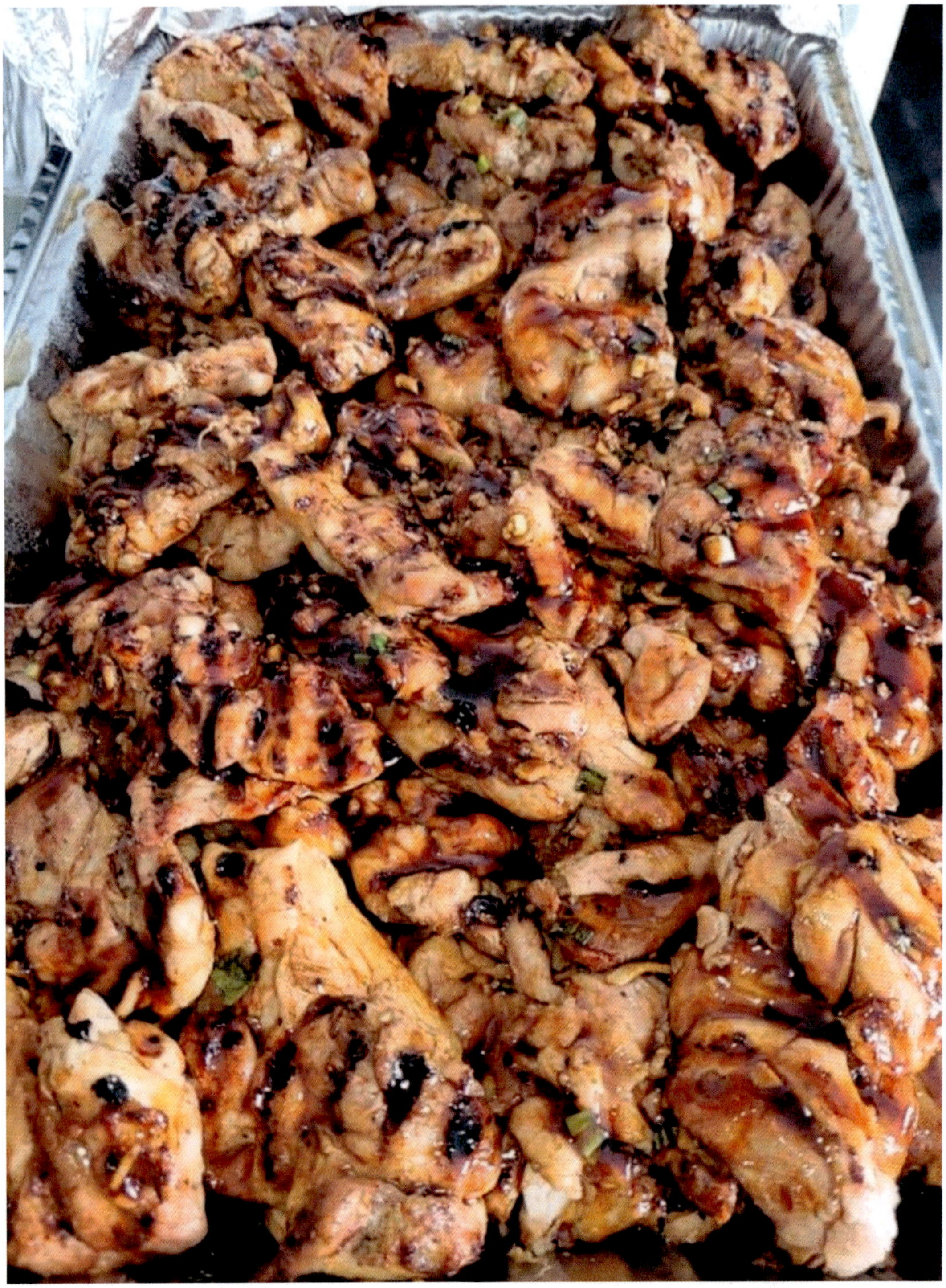

HAWAIIAN SHOYU CHICKEN

This recipe is tried & true. I have used this recipe for many cater jobs as well as my own family Luaus. Its flavor is an explosion to the palette. It's a fun & easy recipe anyone can do. The key here is you use equal parts of the first 3 ingredients. You can double, triple, or even 10x the amount, depending on how much chicken you are going to use.

Ingredients:

- 2 Cups Shoyu (Soy sauce)

- 2 Cups Water

- 2 Cups Granulated sugar

- 1/4 Cup Grated or minced fresh ginger

- 1 Bunch green onions chopped

- 2 Tbsp minced garlic

- Salt & Pepper

- 6 lbs. Boneless skinless leg meat

Directions:

Mix the first 3 ingredients with a whisk until well incorporated, then add the rest of the ingredients and mix well. Set aside.

Clean the chicken leg meat and cut off the tips of the meat where cartilage shows, remove excess skin and toss. Take a gallon zip lock and place the thighs in the bag, add 1/2 cup of the shoyu mix, close the bag and use your hands to gently move the chicken around till well coated. I marinate mine for up to 2 days but you can use the same day. (reserve the rest of the marinade to the side)

Fire up your barbecue and let it get hot. Place flames on medium heat and place the leg meat on the fire. Sear for about 10 minutes and flip the chicken over. Take a brush and dab the seared side with the marinade, then sprinkle with salt & pepper. Repeat this process until the center is cooked and the chicken is nice and glazy. Place the completed chicken in the pan and, pour the marinade over the chicken and place the chicken over foil with plastic in a 350-degree oven for 1 1/2 hours. You can do this in a large skillet, too. Serve my bacon fried rice or even my famous fried rice in this one.

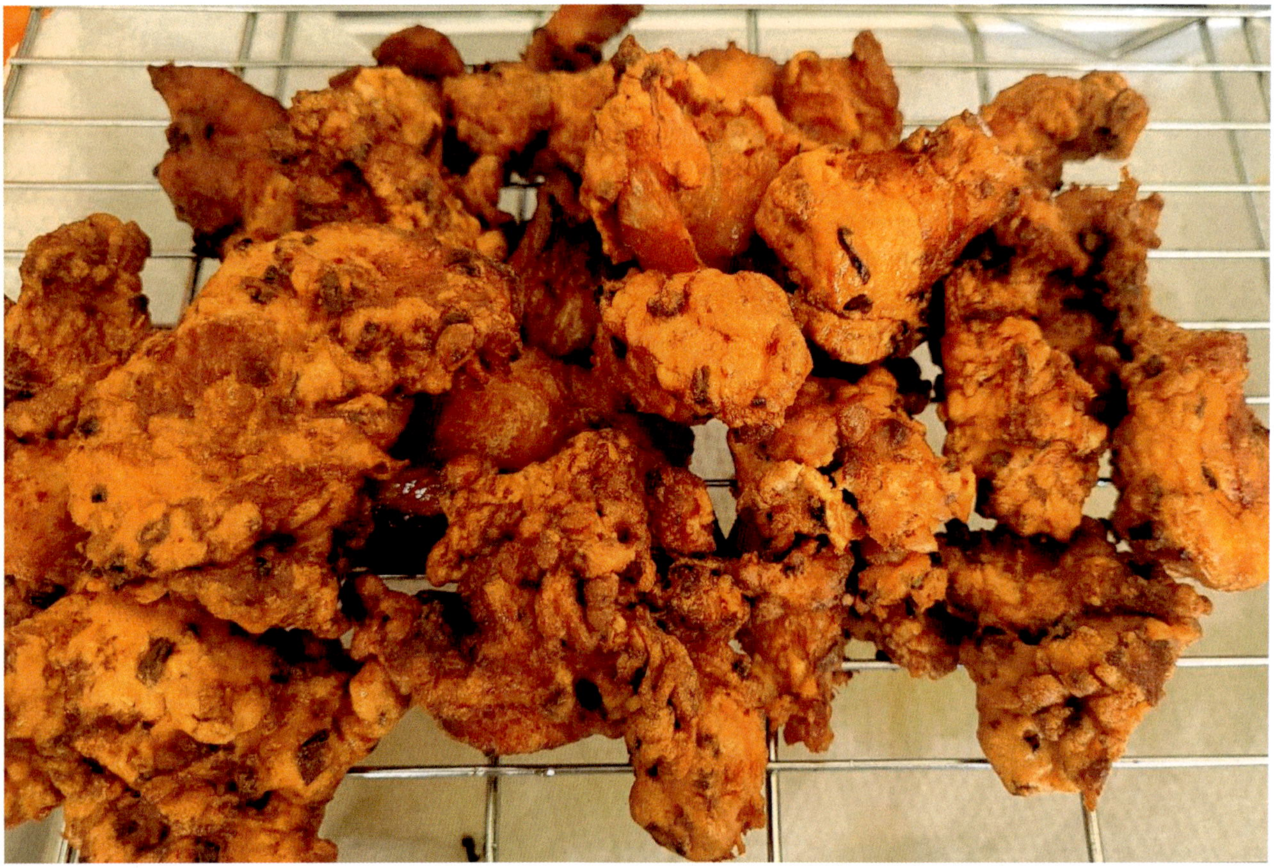

HAWAIIAN MOCHIKO CHICKEN

Ingredients:

- 3 to 4 pounds of boneless skinless leg meat cut into chunks or strips

- 1/3 Cup + 2 Tbsp Granulated sugar

- 1/4 Cup Mochiko (Sweet rice flour can be found in the Asian Aisle in your local grocery market)

- 1/4 Cup Cornstarch

- 1/2 tsp Kosher salt

- 1/2 tsp Black pepper

- 2 Large eggs beaten

- 1/3 Cup sliced green onions

- 4 Tbsp Shoyu (Soy sauce)

- 5 Garlic cloves minced

- 3 Cups vegetable oil for frying

Directions:

Mix sugar, mochiko, cornstarch and salt together in a bowl. Set aside. Whisk eggs and add the green onions, shoyu and garlic together in another bowl. Now, whisk the flour mixture until it forms a smooth batter. Now add the chicken strips or chunks into the batter and cover well. Marinate for at least 5 hours, but overnight is better.

Take a frying pan and, add the vegetable oil and heat over medium heat. Fry the chicken in small batches, being careful not to overcrowd the frying pan. Turn the chicken occasionally until golden brown and the internal temp reads 165 degrees. Drain the chicken on a baking wire rack over a paper towel-lined sheet pan so the chicken stays crispy and doesn't get soft.

COOKING WITH GANAS & ALOHA

ALOHA POKE

Ingredients:

- 2 1/2 Pounds of fresh Ahi tuna cubed

- 1 Maui onion julienned

- 4 stalks of green onions diced

- 1 tsp freshly grated ginger root

- 4 Garlic cloves diced

- 1/2 Cup Shoyu (soy sauce)

- 1 tsp Sesame oil

- 1/2 tsp Oyster sauce

- 1 tsp of Kosher or sea salt

- 2 tsp Sesame seeds (Optional)

Directions:

Cut and cube the tuna and place in a bowl. Season the tuna with the salt and make sure the tuna is completely covered. Add the ginger and mix well again. Add the shoyu, and oyster sauce. Sesame oil and mix thoroughly. The last part is to add the Maui onions, green onions and sesame seeds if you are using them. Refrigerate for at least 1 hour.

If you want the skins still crispy, place a mound of the Poke' on top. I also take 1 large avocado and mash it till creamy, adding salt to taste and add a generous amount of wasabi (depending on how hot you want it) and mix it well into the avocado and add to the plate with the fried wontons and poke' So many people are so please with this version and come back screaming for more.

COOKING WITH GANAS & ALOHA

SAMOAN PALUSAMI

Ingredients:

- 2 15 oz cans of Corned beef (Like Palm brand)

- 2 13.5 oz Coconut cream

- 1 13.6 oz Coconut milk

- 1 Onion diced

- 1 16oz large container fresh spinach plus 1/2 of another Container

- 1 Tbsp salt

- 1 tsp black pepper

Directions:

Take a deep, large baking pan (like 1/2 sheet cake size). Put the diced onion at the bottom of the pan. Next, crumble up the cans of corned beef and lay it on top of the onions. Put 1 can of the coconut cream all over the corned beef with onions. Take some of the spinach and place over the corned beef. Add some of the coconut milk and, pour all over the spinach and repeat the layers until all spinach and coconut milk is used. Now, take the last can of coconut cream and pour it all over the finished spinach. Cover with foil and bake at 350 degrees for 1 hour. Remove from the oven and, add the salt and pepper and stir till all the spinach, onions and corned beef are completely mixed. Serve hot with white rice. Serves about 8 people.

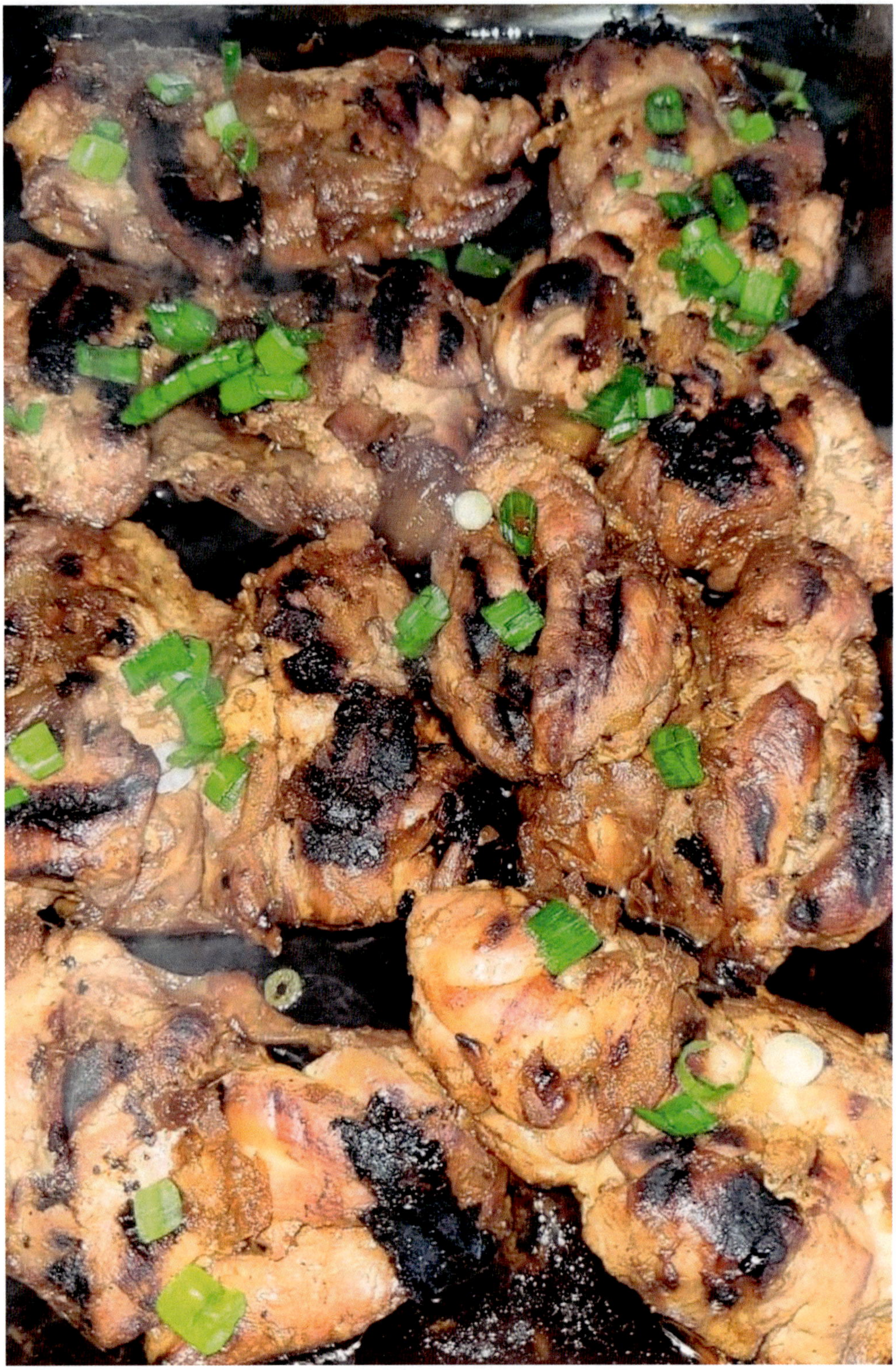

BBQ HULI HULI CHICKEN

Ingredients:

- 1 Cup Firmly packed cup Brown sugar

- 3/4 Cup Ketchup

- 3/4 Cup Low sodium shoyu (Soy sauce)

- 1/3 Cup Chicken broth

- 1 Tbsp freshly grated ginger root

- 1 Tbsp minced garlic

- 1 tsp smoked paprika

- 3 Stalks of green onion sliced thin (garnish)

- 4 Pounds of Boneless skinless thighs

Directions:

In a bowl, mix the first 7 ingredients. (reserve 1 1/2 Cups for basting, cover and refrigerate).

Divide the rest of the sauce into 2 ziplock bags, dividing the chicken thighs between both bags. Refrigerate 6 hours turning the bag every few hours. (It's better to marinate overnight)

Drain and discard the juice from the chicken.

Heat your grill and spray lightly with non-stick cooking spray.

Place your chicken on the grill and cook for about 6 minutes on each side. Baste with the reserved marinade at every turn.

"Huli in Hawaiian means "Turn" a term we use in Hula dancing.

So when you 'Huli' your chicken make sure to dab and baste the chicken. The chicken will be done when the internal temp reaches 165 degrees and the marinade is nice and glazy. Garnish with the cut green onions.

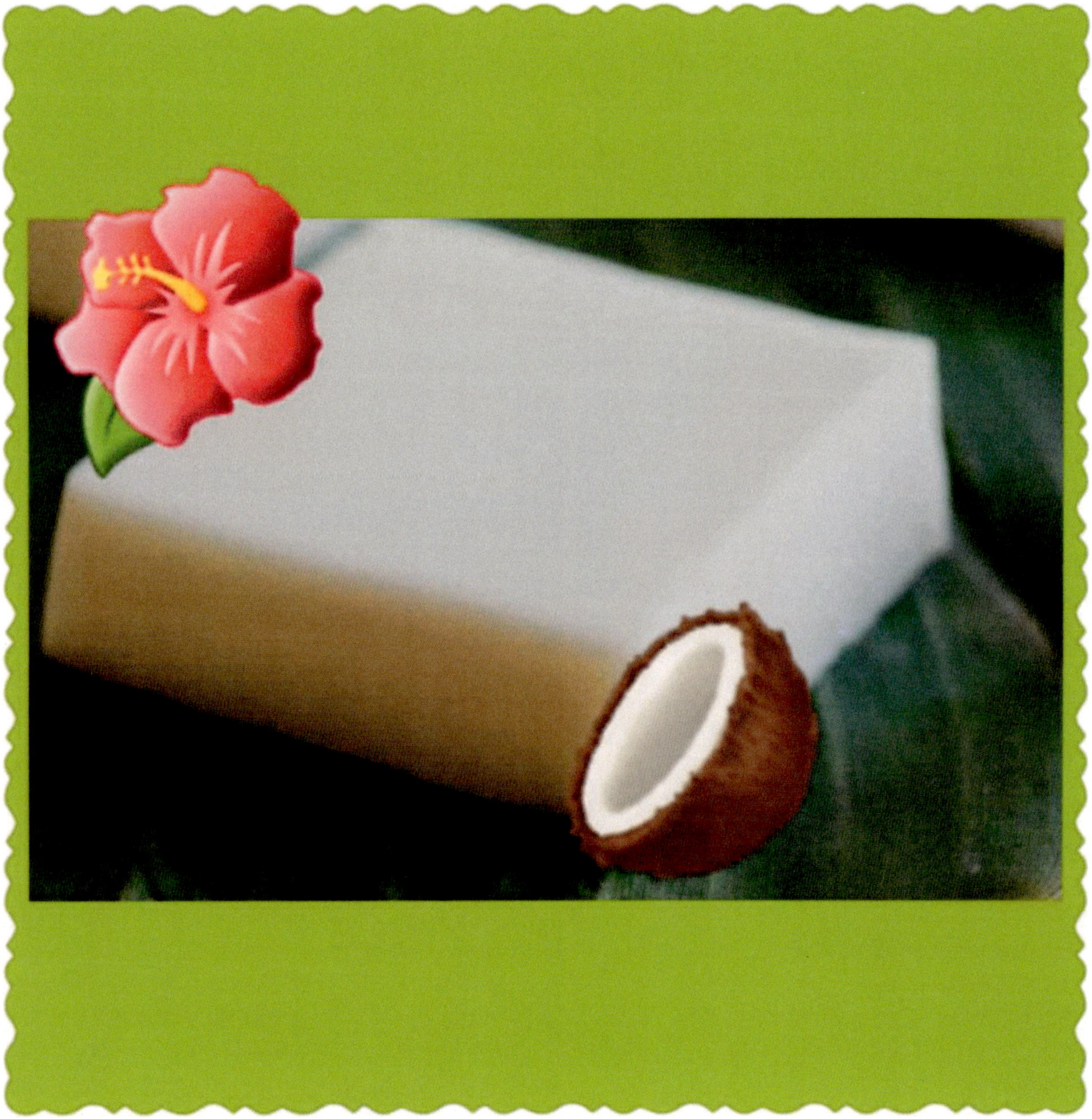

HAUPIA (COCONUT PUDDING DESSERT)

Ingredients:

- 1 Quart Coconut milk

- 1/2 Cup Sugar

- 1/4 Tsp. salt

- 1/3 Cup Shredded coconut

- 1/4 Cup water

- 1/4 Cup Cornstarch

Directions:

Add coconut milk, sugar, and salt to a saucepan and stir over medium heat until sugar dissolves. Reduce heat to low, add coconut and cook for 5 minutes to soften.

In a separate bowl take the water and cornstarch and whisk to make a slurry. Add it into the saucepan and allow to thicken till it's the consistency of yogurt. Transfer to serving dishes and chill. You can pour into a glass pan, chill and cut into squares.

COOKING WITH GANAS & ALOHA

THE QUEENS CHICKEN SALAD

Ingredients:

- 4 Chicken breasts (boiled with salt & pepper and granulated Garlic, cool & shred)
- 1 Stalk of celery chopped
- 1 Whole onion or 2 stalks green onion chopped
- 1 kg Real bacon bits (Not imitation)
- 1 Sm can dice Jalapenos
- 4 shredded carrots
- 1 Head lettuce shredded
- 1 Jar regular mayo
- Coarse black pepper

Directions:

Mix all of the ingredients in a bowl. Add mayo till you get the consistency you want. It should be creamy enough to spread on a tostada shell. Top with your favorite hot sauce. Makes a great summer dinner or a nice potluck dish to take to a party.

COOKING WITH GANAS & ALOHA

DINA'S SHRIMP & CRAB COCKTAIL

Ingredients:

- 5 lbs Cooked, peeled, deveined tail-off shrimp (med. Count)

- 4 lbs Imitation flake style crab meat

- 4 Cucumbers peeled and cut into small chunks

- 6 Fresh yellow chilies, stems off, de-seeded & chopped

- 2 Large white onions diced

- 4 Avocados cut into chunks

- 2 Bunches of rinsed Cilantro chopped

- 2 Large bottles of Clam/tomato juice

- 3 Bottles clam juice

- 4 Fresh squeezed lemon juice

- Granulated garlic to taste

- Ketchup to taste

Directions:

Place all the ingredients in a LARGE bucket or bowl and stir up gently. You can adjust the ketchup and garlic to taste.

Serve in a bowl topped with your favorite hot sauce or on a tostada shell on a hot Summer day.

COOKING WITH GANAS & ALOHA

SOTANGHON (FILIPINO CHICKEN LONG RICE)

Ingredients:

- 4 Chicken breasts (boiled in plenty of water with granulated garlic, salt & pepper, & Ajino moto). You can omit the Ajino moto (MSG) (Do Not discard juice when chicken is done)

- 1 Stalk celery washed and julienned at an angle of about 1/2 inch

- 1 Stalk green onions cut in 1/2 inch pcs.

- 3 Green bell peppers cut in half and sliced diagonally into strips

- 1 Sm can of mushroom pieces and stems

- 1 Sm jar pimentos

- 1 Pkg of bean thread (Vermicelli) found at Filipino Mrkt.

- Soy sauce to taste

Directions:

Cook the chicken breast & shred them chunky and place them back into the broth. Add all the remaining ingredients except the vermicelli. Add soy sauce to taste.

Place the pkg. of vermicelli in a bowl of warm water till noodles soften and cut with scissors in long noodles. (Don't over-cut too small) Drain and place noodles in the pot with other ingredients. Cook until noodles turn clear. Serve over a scoop of white rice.

If you need to add more juice, you can add more chicken broth.

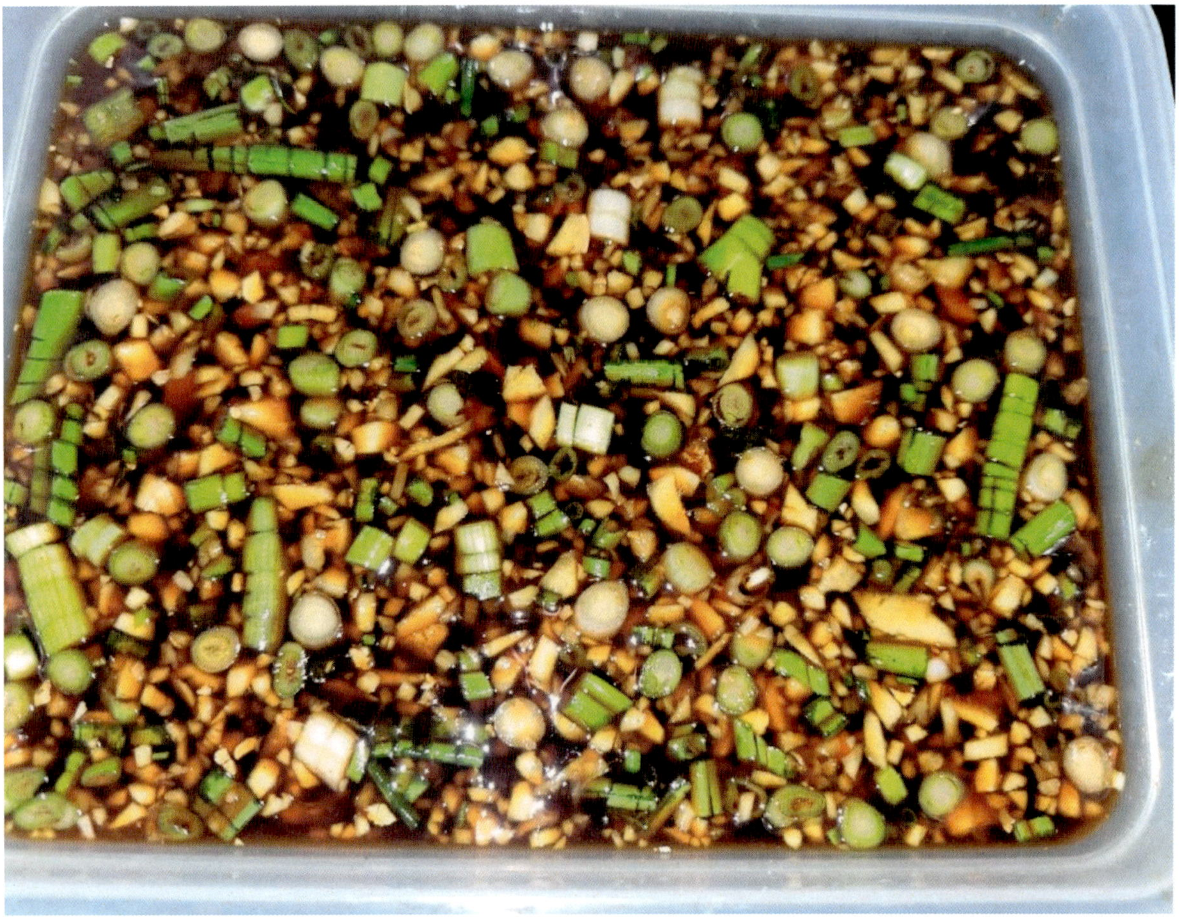

MY SECRET TERIYAKI SAUCE

Ingredients:

- 8 Cups Soy Sauce

- 2 Cans Pineapple juice

- 1 1/2 lbs Brown sugar

- 2 16 oz Light karo syrup (The secret to make it sticky)

- 2 Bunches Green onion chopped (save 3 Tbsp for garnish)

- 1 Large Ginger root peeled and chopped or grated

- 1 Whole garlic bulb chopped fine (probably 6 cloves)

- Coarse black pepper

- 1 package of Sesame seeds optional (I don't use them)

Directions:

Mix all the ingredients together.

Directions for Meat marinade:

Marinate your chicken/meat (Boneless leg meat works best, juicy, not dry like breast) in a portion of the sauce in a zip lock for 24 hours 48 is better. When grilling, discard the juice from the zip lock and use the extra sauce to baste. Keep some extra sauce to add to your pan when you bake chicken; pour it all over the chicken and add a cup of water to the bottom of the pan, cover with foil and cook for 2 hours till steamy and hot. Garnish with chopped green onions & Serve.

COOKING WITH GANAS & ALOHA

HAWAIIAN POTATO MAC SALAD

Ingredients:

1 16 oz Bag or box of small elbow macaroni boiled and drained

3 Lrg Baking potatoes boiled till soft and peeled (keep hot)

1 Doz Large eggs boiled and peeled & chopped

1 Stalk celery (diced)

1 Stalk green onions (Chopped)

2 Carrots grated

8 oz Small Jar light Mayo

1 30 oz Jar regular mayo

Salt & pepper to taste

Directions:

In a large bowl, place the drained & rinsed macaroni; add the celery, Green Onions, carrots, and eggs. Add the hot chopped potatoes and lay them on top of the ingredients in a bowl. Salt & pepper the potatoes lightly don't over salt because the mayo is salty; add the light mayo and gently toss the potatoes, add the regular mayo and toss it into all the ingredients in the bowl. It should be moist, not dry, and you can add more because if it sits overnight, it will absorb the mayo. At this point, you can add more salt & pepper to taste. If you over salt add another potato. Garnish the top with sprinkled paprika. If you 3x's this recipe it will fill one full size foil catering pan.

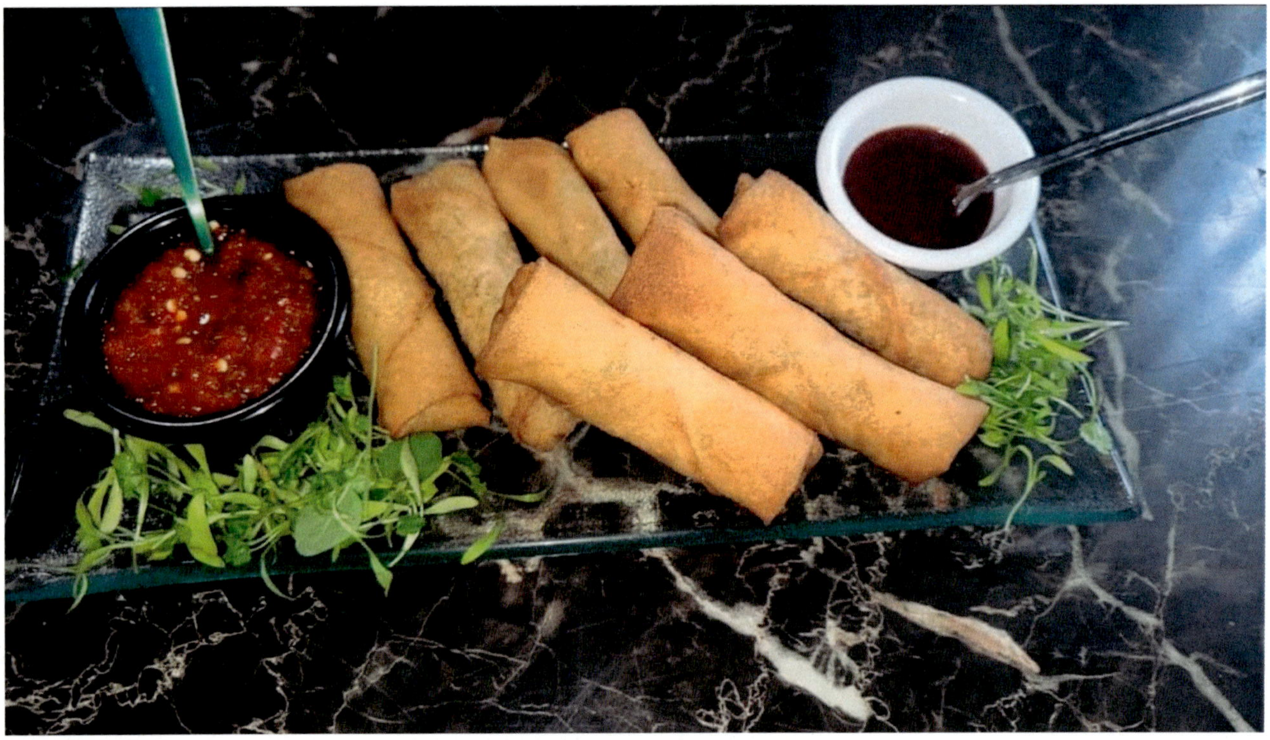

PORK WITH VEGGIE LUMPIA

Ingredients:

1 Small boneless pork butt

2 Celery stalks rinsed and diced

3 Bunches green onions chopped

3 Large baking potatoes peeled and diced

4 Large carrots grated or bag shredded carrots

1 Can whole kernel corn

1 Can French-style green beans

2 lbs Bean sprouts

1 Medium head of green cabbage shredded

1-40 pack Lumpia wrappers (I use Dynasty or Menlo) Found at your local Filipino market.

Directions:

Place all ingredients into the pot with the meat & juice and boil till the veggies are cooked. DO NOT overcook. Drain well thru a colander. Let it cool completely; refrigeration is better. Re-drain before use. Take 1 egg and scramble in a small bowl with a fork set aside. Peel wrappers apart, and place 1 heaping Tbsp of mix and place in the corner of the wrapper closest to you. Roll firmly and, bring in the side flaps and continue to roll. Place a small amt of egg wash to seal the wrapper. Fry and drain. Enjoy with your favorite dipping sauce. Sauce: Mix 1/2 soy sauce 1/2 vinegar.

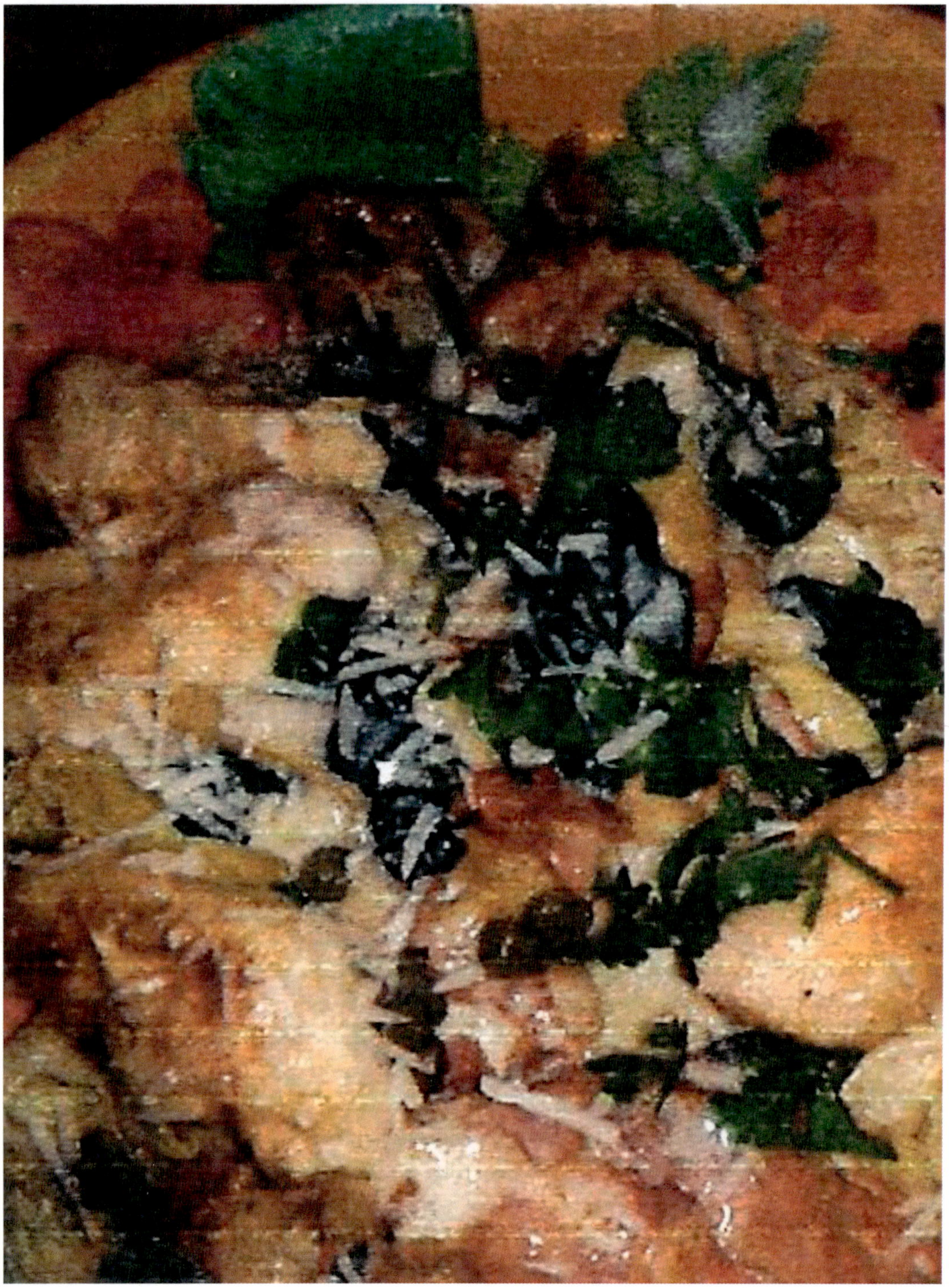

CHICKEN SCALLOPINI

(COPY CAT RECIPE) PART I

Ingredients for Lemon Butter sauce:

4 Oz Lemon juice

2 Oz. White wine

4 Oz Heavy Cream

1 Lb Butter (4 Sticks)

Ingredients for Chicken & Pasta:

6-8 Chicken breasts

Oil for sautéing

2 3/4 Cups flour (Seasoned with salt & Pepper for dredging)

6 oz Pancetta, Cooked

12 Oz Mushrooms sliced

12 oz Artichoke hearts

1 Tbsp capers

1 Lb Cappellini pasta

Chopped parsley for garnish

Directions:

To make the sauce, heat the lemon juice and white wine in a saucepan. Bring to a boil & reduce by 1/3. Add cream and simmer till thickens (3 to 4 minutes). Slowly add the butter whisk till completely incorporated. Season to taste with salt & pepper. Remove from heat and keep warm. Note I double the recipe for sauce because we pour more over the finished product. This recipe is tried & true and my favorite of The Macaroni Grill.

PART II

Directions:

To make the chicken & pasta: Cook the pasta and drain Heat 2 TBSP butter in a large skillet Cut the chicken breasts into sliced cutlets and dredge in the salt & pepper flour mixture and place in the oil in the skillet, turning once until browned and cooked through. Remove chicken from the pan. Add the remaining ingredients to the skillet and heat until the mushrooms soften and are cooked. Add the chicken back to the skillet. Place cooked pasta on each plate and add half the lemon butter sauce to the chicken mixture and toss till well coated. Taste and adjust. (Add more sauce to each plate) Garnish with parsley. Note: I pour extra sauce in a small condiment dish and serve on the plate next to the pasta. Note You won't be disappointed!

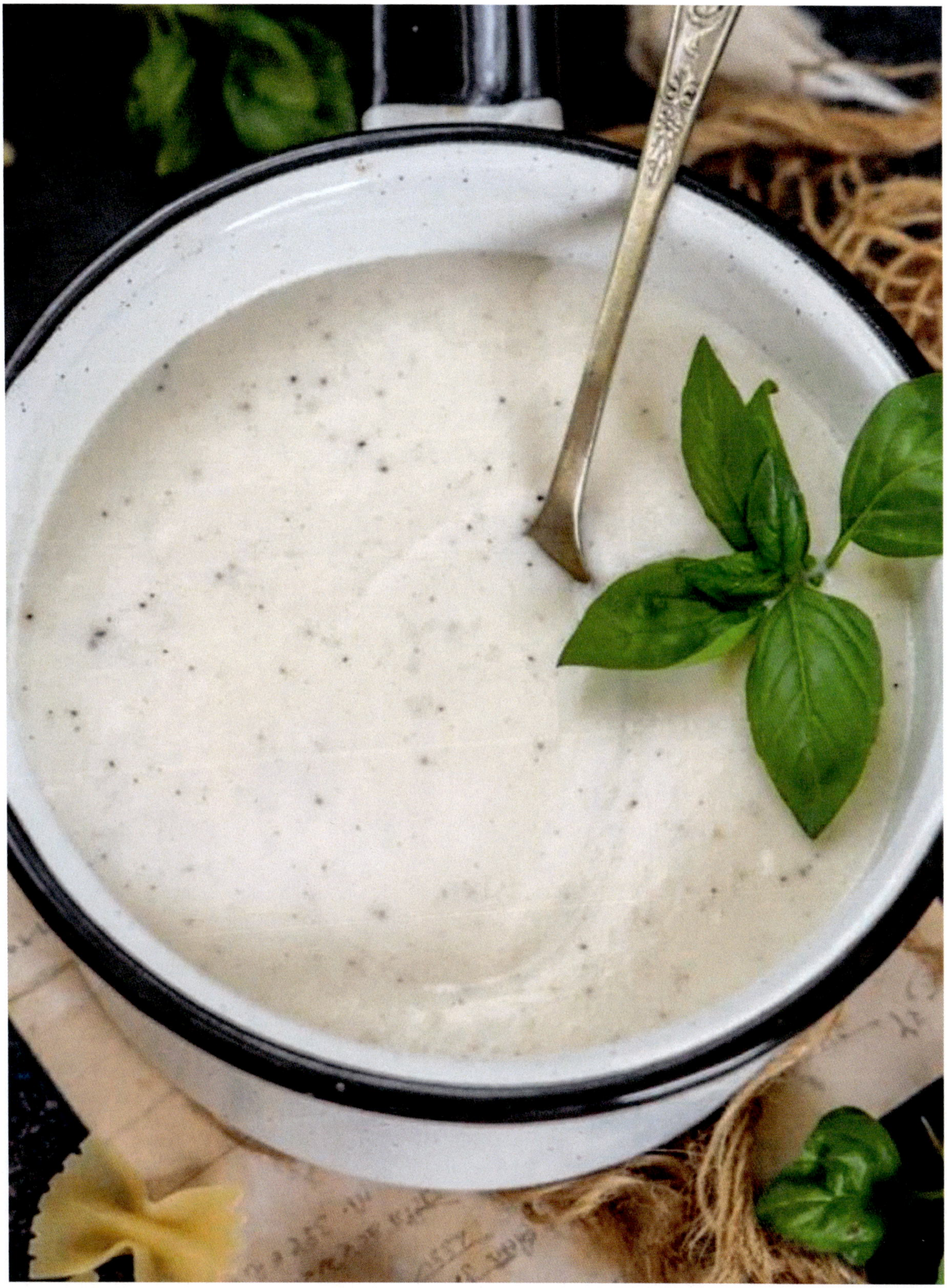

ROUX BASIC WHITE SAUCE

Ingredients:

1 Stick Butter or margarine

1/3 Cup Flour

3 Cups Milk

Salt & pepper to taste

Directions:

In a deep frying pan, melt butter, then Whisk in the flour till pasty. Whisk in Milk and rapidly whisk while pouring to get all lumps out. You can add more milk if needed to the thickened consistency you desire. Once whisked, add salt to taste. The sauce will thicken as it keeps cooking make sure to lower the heat and add milk till you get it to your desired thickness. NOTE: This Roux is used for gravies and a basic for Alfredo sauce, Cheese sauce and Clam chowder, gumbo, etc., which you will find in my other recipes. Always come back to this recipe as your basic. I have also used vegetable oil instead of butter or margarine.

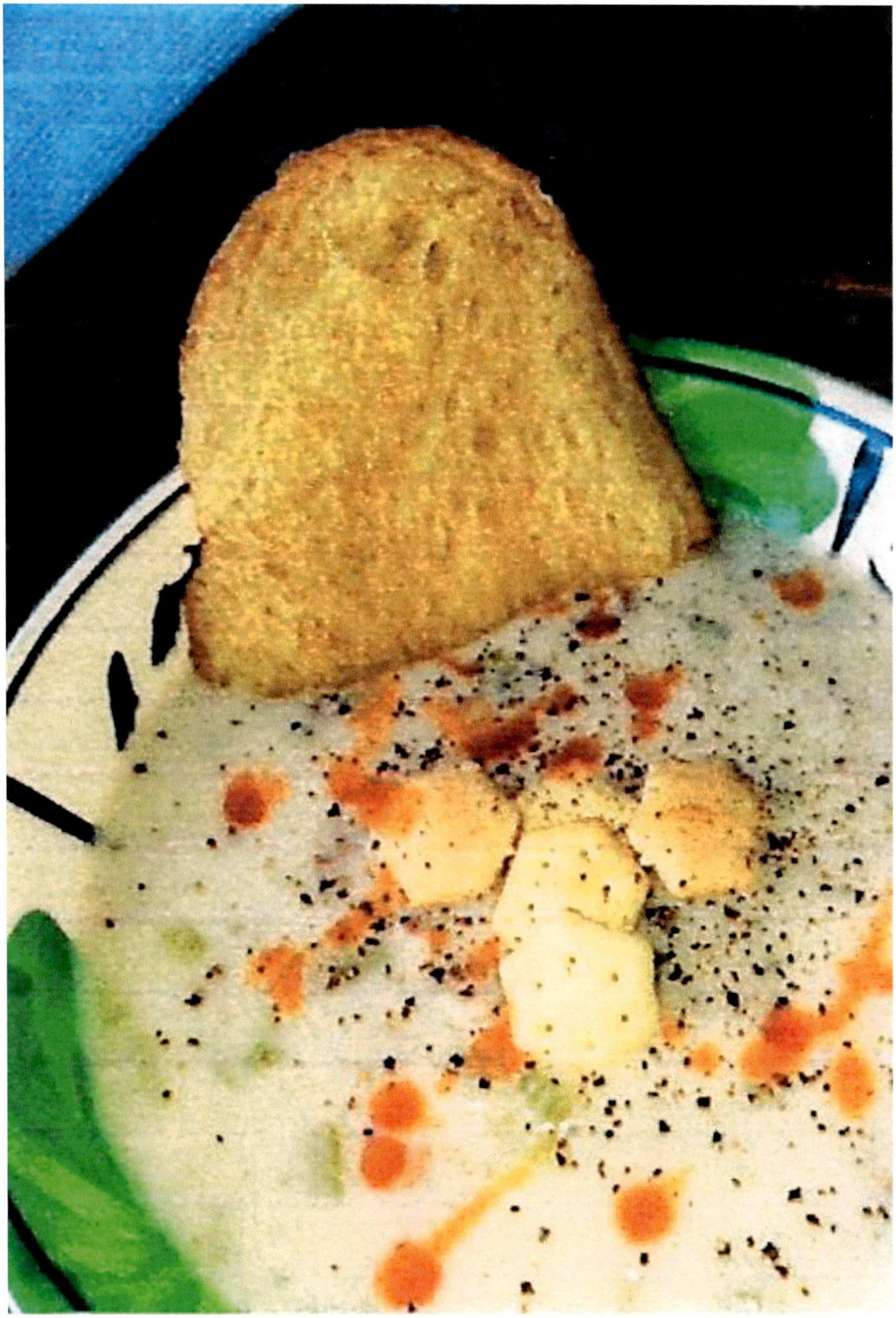

MY CLAM CHOWDER

Ingredients:

1 lb Bacon cut into small pieces

1 White onion diced

3 Baking potatoes diced

4 Cans of chopped clams

6 Celery ribs diced

1 Bottle of clam juice

Salt & pepper to taste

Whole Milk

Directions:

Make your basic Roux (White sauce). Set aside (The recipe for roux is in this cookbook). In a soup or stock pot, place the bacon and fry till it's almost crisp. Add the chopped onion and cook till the onion is caramelized. Remove the fat and put it in a bowl to the side. Add the potatoes, Cans of clams (juice, too), celery and bottle of clam juice into the pot & stir all together. Add the Roux mix and whisk till it's all creamy and mixed together. Salt & pepper to taste. If the soup is thick, you can add milk to thin it out to the consistency you want. Serve with warm sourdough bread or place soup in a sourdough bowl scooped out. Reserve the center of the bowl to dip into the soup

COOKING WITH GANAS & ALOHA

CHILI BEANS

Ingredients:

2 lbs Pinto Beans (washed and cooked, save juice)

1 lb Hamburger

1 lb Pork sausage (I use hot)

1 Medium Onion chopped

1 Tbsp Granulated or chopped garlic

1 Tbsp Coarse black pepper

1 Tbsp Salt

1 Tbsp Ground cumin

1 3 oz Package Dry California ground chili (You can use New Mexico chili if you want it spicier)

1 15 oz Can whole tomatoes

1 15 oz Can of tomato sauce

1 Small can of diced Ortega chiles

Directions:

In a large frying pan, combine the hamburger, Pork sausage, and Onion and fry till almost done. Drain fat. Add all the seasonings above except chili powder. Mix in thoroughly. Next, add the whole can of tomatoes and gently pull the tomatoes apart with your fingers; add the tomato sauce and Chili powder and Ortega's; it will be pasty. Next, add the Chili mixture to your pot of beans and mix well. At this point, you can add some juice from the beans to make it soupier if desired. Adjust your salt and add more ground chili for a richer taste. (I add about 1/4 Cup Honey BBQ sauce and about 3 TBSP of Tabasco for a real good taste) You can omit the beans and just use the chili straight. Really good on hot dogs!

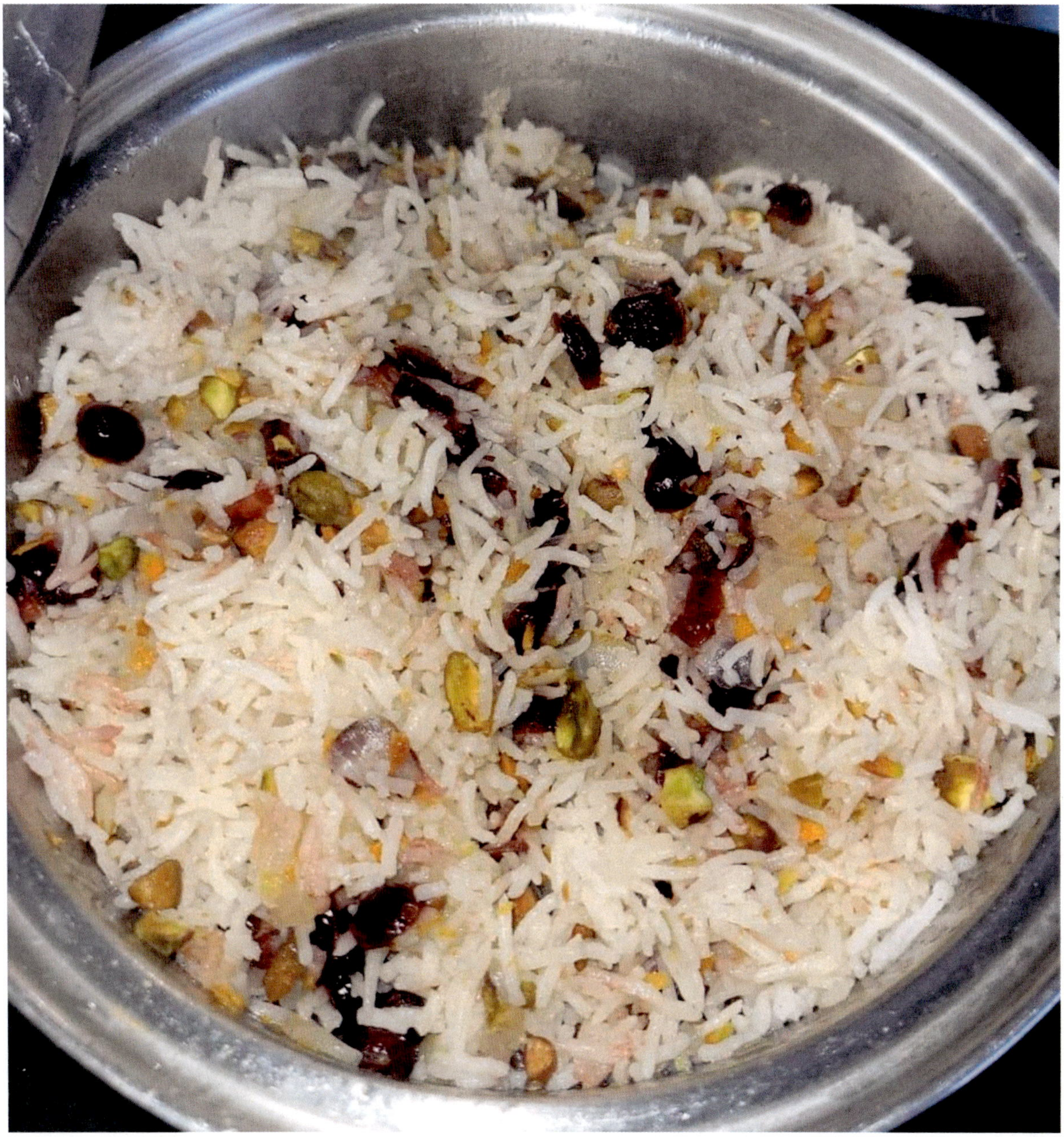

CRANBERRY PISTACHIO BASMATI RICE

Ingredients:

2 Cups Basmati rice

1 Small onion diced

2 tbsp Honey

4 Cups Chicken broth or water

1/2 tsp Cumin

1/2 tsp Black pepper

1/2 Cup dried cranberries

1/3 Cup Chopped, peeled & salted pistachio's

2 Tbsp Orange zest

1 Tsp Chopped parsley

Directions:

Rinse the rice until the water is clear. Using a pot with a tight-fitting lid, bring the broth or water to a boil, and lower the flame to medium (Do NOT use a lid with a vent hole). Add the rice, onion, cumin, honey, salt & pepper and stir. Cook on medium heat until the liquid is about even with the rice, about 15 minutes. Shut the flame off and let the rice continue to steam in the pot for another 15 minutes. IMPORTANT: Do NOT lift the lid during the steaming Process. After 15 minutes, lift the lid; the rice should be fluffy. Mix in the cranberries and pistachios and fluff with a fork. Put the lid back on for another 5 minutes. Garnish with the orange zest and parsley. Serve warm.

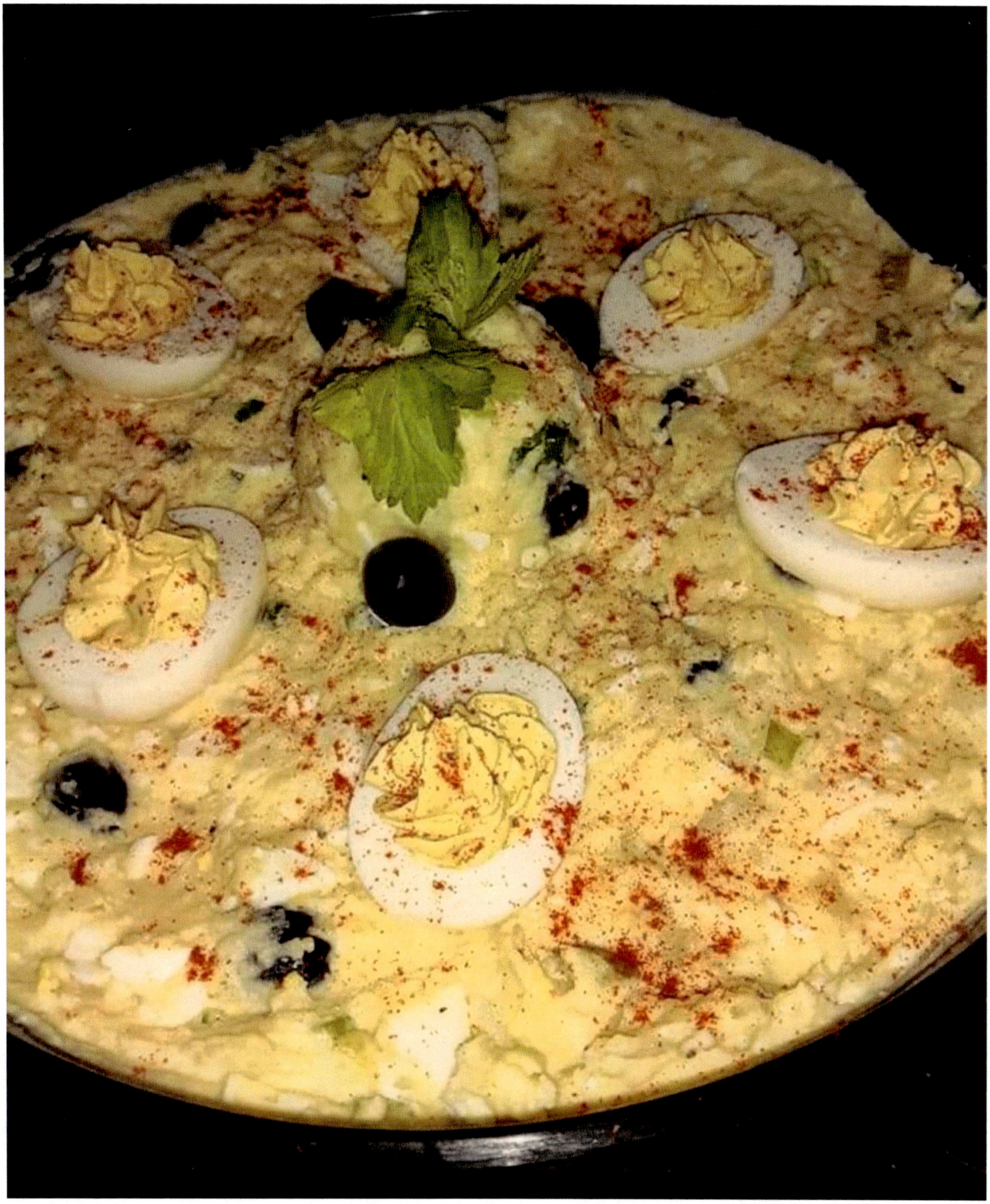

MY FINEST POTATO SALAD

Ingredients:

1 10 lb Bag Russet potatoes

1 Bunch celery chopped

2 Bunch Green onions chopped

18 Eggs hard boiled, peeled and chopped (Reserve 3 eggs)

6 Dill pickle spears juice squeezed out & chopped (Optional)

1 Can medium black olives drained (whole, sliced or chopped)

1 64 oz jar best Foods mayo

Mustard for color

Salt & pepper to taste

Directions:

Boil the potatoes till a knife is inserted and soft. (Do not overcook or they will fall apart to mush) Run the potatoes under cold water till cool to the touch, but the potatoes should still be warm. Peel and cut them into 2-inch chunks; add a little salt and pepper to the potatoes and toss; now add some mayo to coat the potatoes (Do not over salt because the mayo is salty). Add the rest of the ingredients and mix well with your hands until the potatoes are no longer chunky. Add the mayo a little at a time and squeeze a little mustard for color. The Potato salad should have a moist and creamy texture. If you are making this a day ahead, the potatoes will absorb the mayo and you may have to add more the next day. Garnish with the 3 eggs halved and sprinkle with paprika. Note: Be sure to add enough salt & mayo at the end; there's nothing worse than a dry, tasteless potato salad!

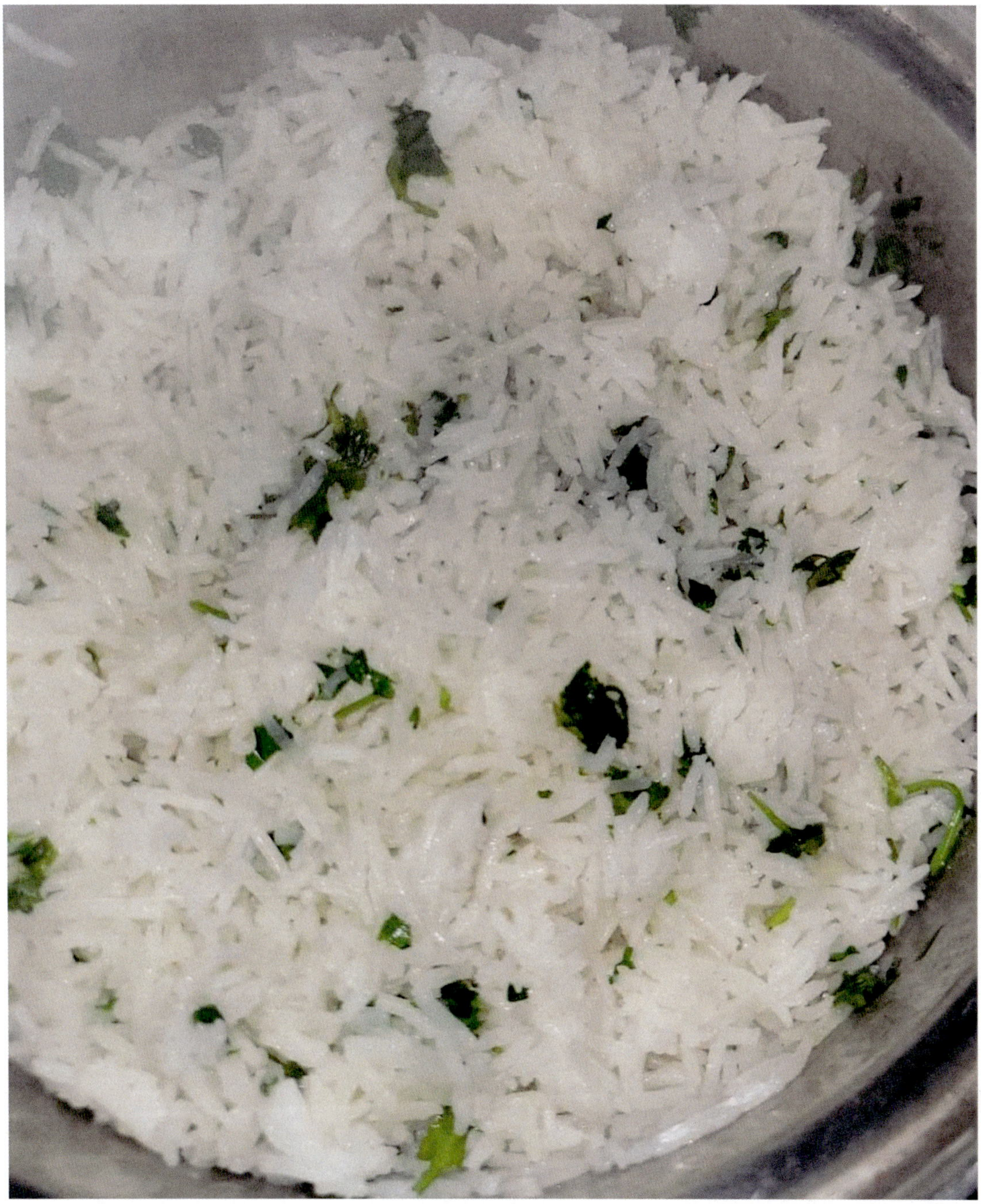

CILANTRO LIME BASMATI RICE

Ingredients:

1 Cup Basmati rice

2 Cups Water

2 Tbsp Butter

2 tsp Salt

1 Whole Lime juice squeezed (I like using 2 limes)

3 TBSP fresh chopped cilantro

Directions:

Rinse the rice well and place in a bowl to side. Bring the water to a boil; add the salt, lime juice and butter till melted; stir in the rice, lower the flame to low, put the cover on and simmer for 20 min. Do Not lift the lid during the cooking time. After 20 min shut the flame off and let the rice steep for 5 min. Remove the lid and gently mix in the cilantro with a fork. Serve hot. Cook Time: 20 Minutes Makes 2 Cups

COOKING WITH GANAS & ALOHA

JALAPENO HUMMUS

Ingredients:

2 15 oz Cans of chick peas (garbanzo beans) Drained but save the liquid

5 Cloves of garlic

2/3 Cups of tahini

1 Bunch of fresh cilantro stems off

1/4 Cup fresh squeezed lemon juice

1/4 Cup Olive oil

1 tsp cumin

1 tsp black pepper

4 jalapenos stems off, deseeded and diced (You can use 2 jalapenos for a less spicy hummus). You can add 1 whole avocado if you wish

Directions:

Place all of the ingredients into a blender or food processor, add about 1/4 cup of the chick pea juice and blend on high till creamy. You can add a little more juice until you get the consistency you want. Store in an airtight container. Chill for about 1 hour before serving. You can garnish with fresh sprigs of cilantro and sliced or diced jalapenos. Serve with warm pita bread or pita chips. It's guiltless on celery sticks.

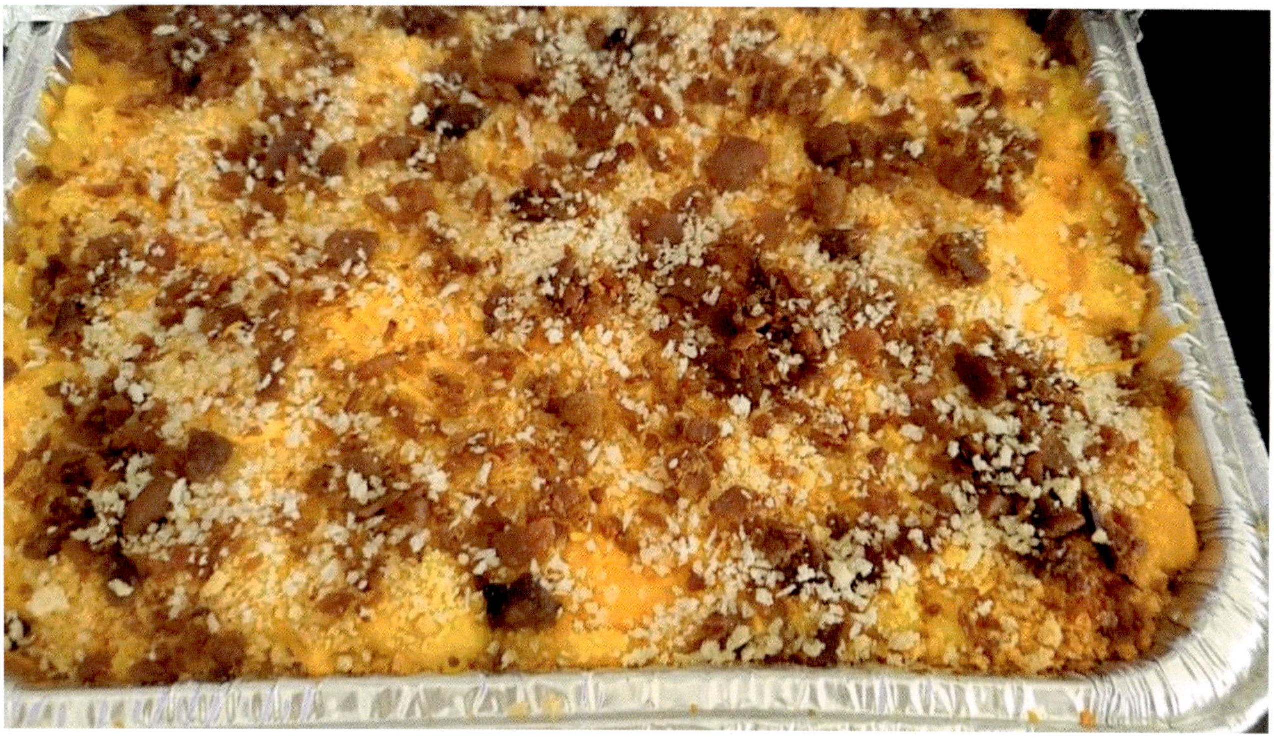

COOKING WITH GANAS & ALOHA

INSANE MAC N CHEESE

Ingredients:

1 lb of Small elbow macaroni

1 Small block of boxed melting cheese cut into squares

1 lb Mild cheddar cheese grated (Save 1/2 Cup to the side)

3 Tbsp Mustard

Salt to taste

Milk

1/2 Cup Bread crumbs

Basic white roux sauce found in this cookbook

Directions:

Boil and drain the macaroni and place in a casserole dish or pan. Add the mustard to the macaroni until well coated. Make the basic white roux sauce. While in the skillet add the boxed melting cheese until well incorporated. Next, add the cheddar cheese and whisk until melted and creamy. You can add some milk if it's too thick. Now pour the cheese sauce into the macaroni and mix until well incorporated. Top the coated macaroni with the 1/2 cup of cheddar cheese and the bread crumbs. Cover with a lid or foil and bake for 45 minutes at 350 degrees. Be careful when removing the lid or foil; it will be very hot. This is so cheesy and insanely good. You can add some bacon crumbles on top, too. It adds a great flavor or I've added some habanero powder for a real spicy kick.

COOKING WITH GANAS & ALOHA

COOKING WITH GANAS & ALOHA

COLORFUL JELLO COOKIES

Ingredients:

1/2 Cup Butter

1/2 Cup Granulated sugar

1 Egg

1 1/2 Cups All-purpose flour

1/2 tsp Baking soda

1/2 tsp Baking powder

3 small boxes of different flavored Jello

Instructions:

1. Preheat your oven to 350 degrees.

2. Cream together the butter, sugar, and eggs.

3. Incorporate the baking soda and baking powder into the flour mix well.

4. Add the flour to the Creamed mixture and mix until dough forms.

5. Divide the dough into 3 parts. Add 5 tsp of Jello powder to each portion, along with about 4 drops of matching food coloring. Knead until the dough is colored. You can add more food coloring for a deeper color if you wish.

6. Roll the dough into 1" balls and place on a parchment-lined baking sheet. Take the bottom of a glass and gently press on the dough to flatten slightly.

7. Bake for about 10 minutes, let cool for 2 minutes and place on a cooling rack until completely cooled.

8. (I have also sprinkled a little sugar on top of cookies before baking to add a sugary effect)

COOKING WITH GANAS & ALOHA

MY BEST OATMEAL RAISIN COOKIES

Ingredients:

3/4 Cup butter softened

3/4 Cup Granulated sugar

3/4 Cup Brown sugar

2 Eggs

1 tsp Vanilla

1 1/4 Cup Flour

1 tsp Baking soda

1 TBSP Cinnamon

1/2 tsp Salt

2 3/4 Cups Rolled oats

1 Cup Raisins

Directions:

Preheat oven to 350 degrees.

In a large bowl, cream together the butter and sugars until smooth.

Beat in eggs and vanilla till fluffy.

In another bowl, stir together flour, soda, cinnamon, and salt.

Gradually beat it into the butter mixture. Stir in oats and raisins.

Drop by teaspoon fulls onto ungreased cookie sheets 2 inches apart.

Bake for 8 to 10 minutes until golden brown. Cool slightly on a wire rack till cooled completely.

COOKING WITH GANAS & ALOHA

CRUNCHY PEANUT BUTTER COOKIES

Ingredients:

1 Cup White sugar

1/2 Cup Firmly packed brown sugar

1/2 Cup Butter or margarine

1/2 Cup Crunchy or creamy peanut butter

1 Large egg

1/2 tsp Vanilla extract

1 1/2 Cup All-purpose flour

1/2 tsp Salt

1/2 tsp Baking soda

Directions:

1. Heat oven to 400 degrees.
2. In a mixing bowl with an electric mixer, cream the sugars with butter and peanut butter until light & fluffy.
3. Beat the egg and vanilla into the creamed mixture until smooth and well blended.
4. In a separate bowl, combine the flour, salt, and soda and mix well.
5. Add it to the creamed mixture gradually.
6. Using lightly floured hands, shape the dough into 1-inch balls and place 2" apart on an ungreased cookie sheet.
7. Dip a fork into flour and press into the dough, making a crisscross pattern (dip the fork in white sugar)
8. Bake for about 7-10 minutes or until cookies are lightly golden brown around the edges. Cool on the wire rack. Store in airtight containers.

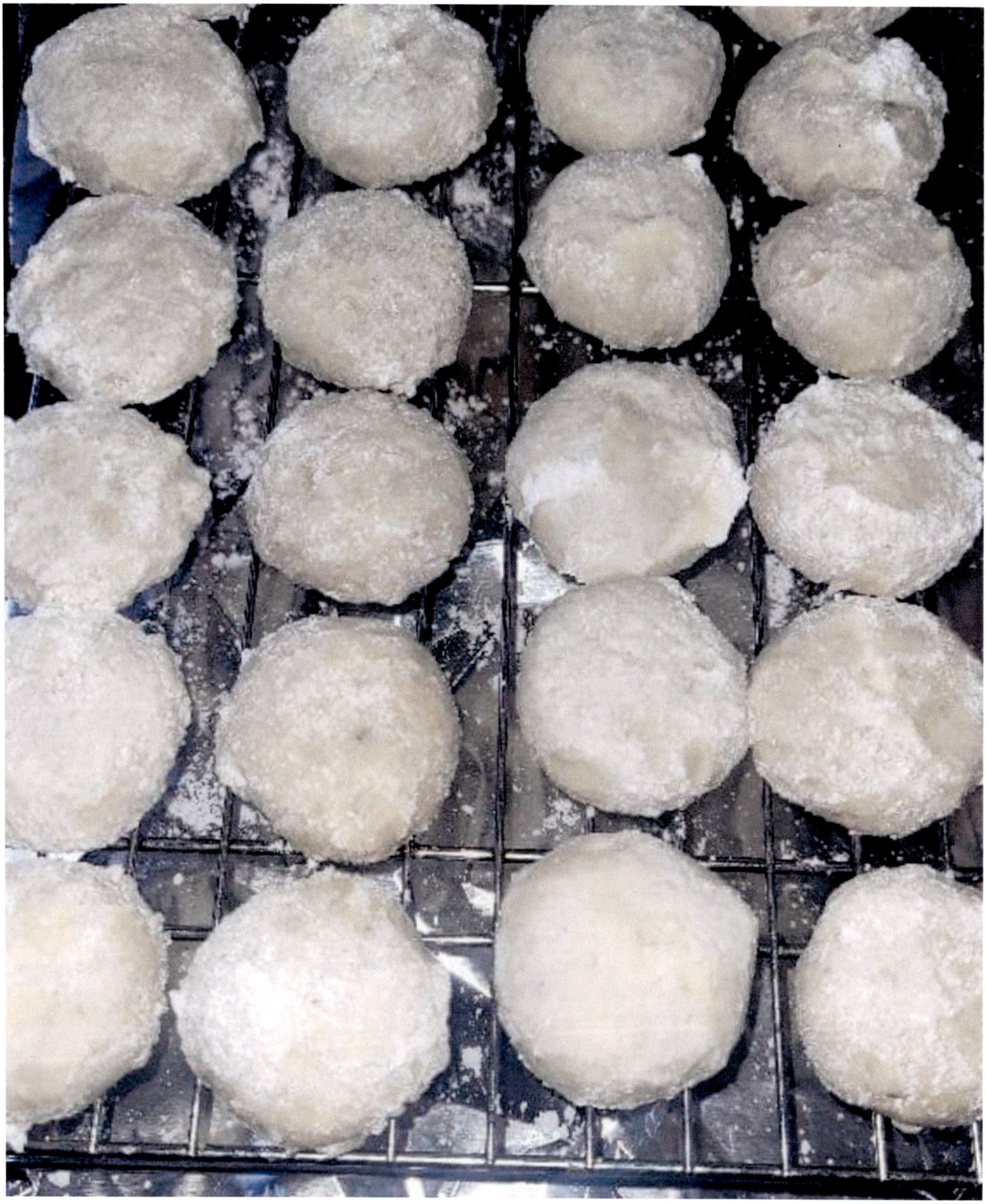

SNOWBALLS, AKA MEXICAN WEDDING COOKIES

Ingredients:

- 1 Cup Margarine or butter
- 5 Tbsp Powdered sugar
- 1/2 Cup Chopped pecans
- 2 Cups Flour
- 2 tsp Vanilla

Directions:

1. Mix all the above ingredients till they form into a dough.
2. Roll into balls about 1"
3. Place on an ungreased cookie sheet and bake at 350 degrees till lightly brown.
4. Remove and roll into a bowl of powdered sugar. Place on a wire rack till cools or the bottoms get gummy.
5. After cooling, I sprinkle more powdered sugar into the bowl with the cookies.

COOKING WITH GANAS & ALOHA

COOKING WITH GANAS & ALOHA

PEAR SQUARES

Ingredients:

1/2 Cup Margarine

1 tsp. Vanilla

3/4 Cup Flour

1/2 Cup Chopped walnuts

1/4 Cup Granulated sugar

Directions:

Mix all ingredients together and press into the bottom of a sprayed-coated pan.

Bake for about 20 min at 350 degrees.

Now mix:

2- 8 oz Boxes of cream cheese

2 Eggs

2 tsp Vanilla

1/4 Cup Sugar and beat till creamy

Spread the mixture on the crust. Add 1 very well-drained can sliced pears across the whole top of the mixture, sprinkle with cinnamon and bake at 350 for 30 min. Let cool completely. Cool and cut into squares. Refrigerate. Serve in cupcake liners. This recipe is one of my favorites.

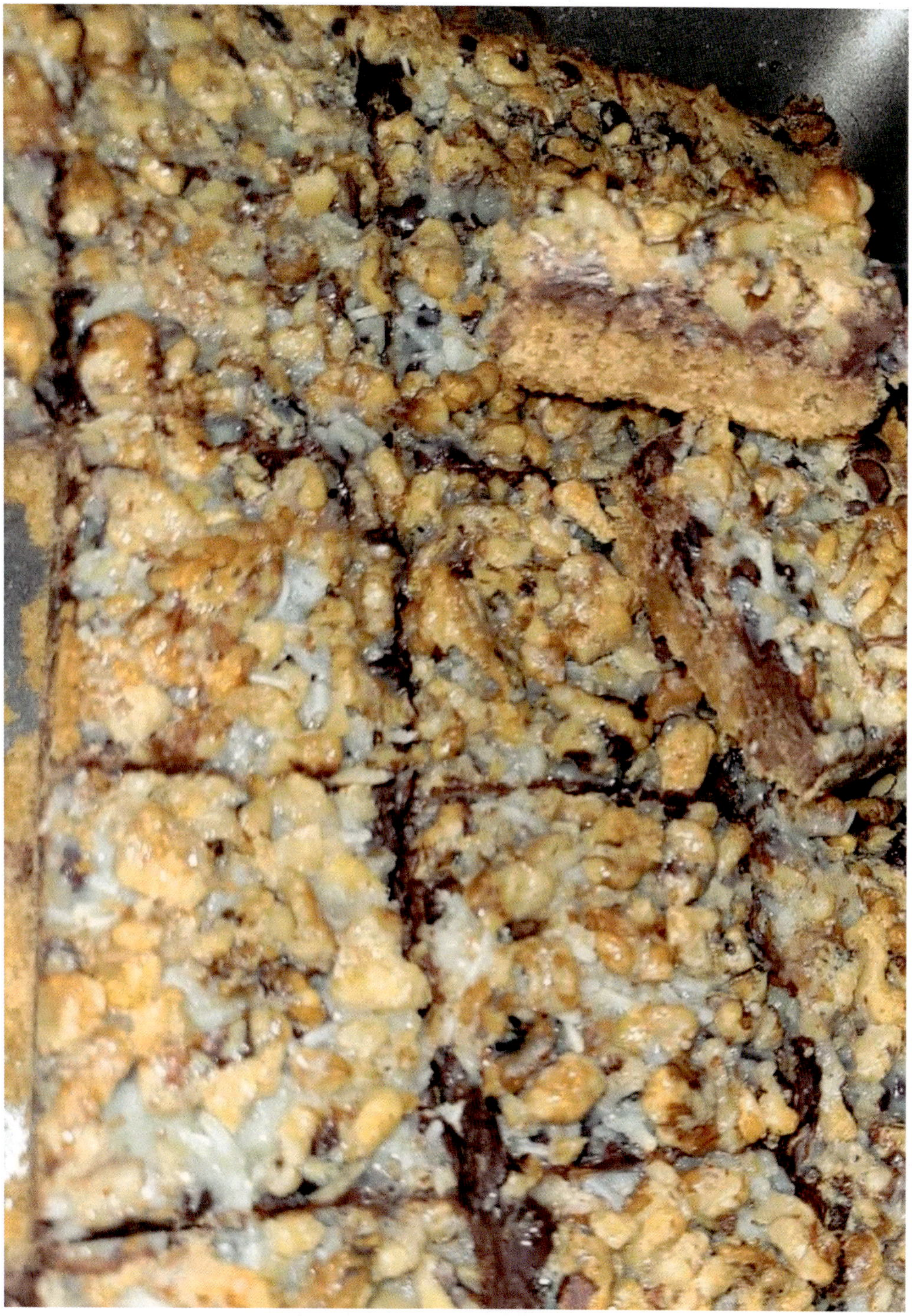

COOKING WITH GANAS & ALOHA

COCONUT CHEWY'S

Ingredients:

1 Cube Butter

1 Cup Graham cracker crumbs

12 oz Bag Chocolate chips

1 Cup Shredded coconut

1 Cup Chopped walnuts

1 Can Sweet condensed milk

Directions:

1. Melt butter and mix in a bowl with the graham cracker crumbs
2. Press in the bottom of a 9x13 inch pan.
3. Sprinkle top with the coconut and chocolate chips.
4. Pour 1/2 of the milk over the top.
5. Now sprinkle the nuts all over the top of that and then pour the rest of the milk over the nuts.
6. Bake at 350 degrees for 30 minutes. Let it cool completely and cut it into squares.
7. This recipe is delectable and gets many likes and loves.

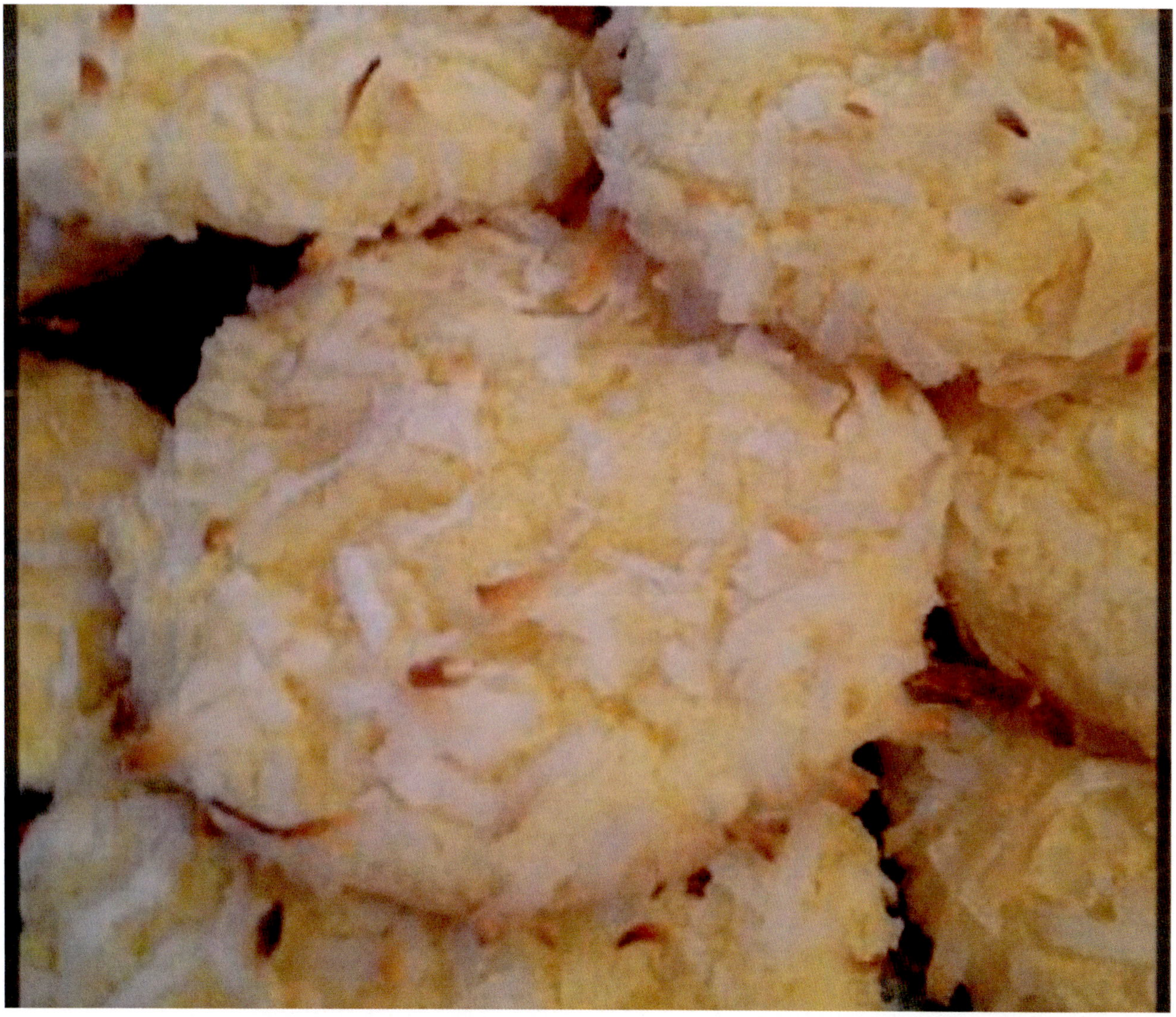

COCONUT CLOUDS

Ingredients:

1 Box Vanilla cake mix

1 Egg

1/2 Cup Oil

1/4 Cup water

1 1/4 Tsp. Vanilla extract

1 1/3 Cup flaked Coconut

Directions:

Mix all the ingredients except the coconut. After you have mixed all the ingredients, stir in the coconut and roll into 1" balls then roll it in more coconut. Place on cookie sheet 2" apart. Bake at 350 for 15 min. Do not over bake. Let cool for 10 min. and move to a cooling rack to completely cool. This is an incredibly easy recipe and loved by many.

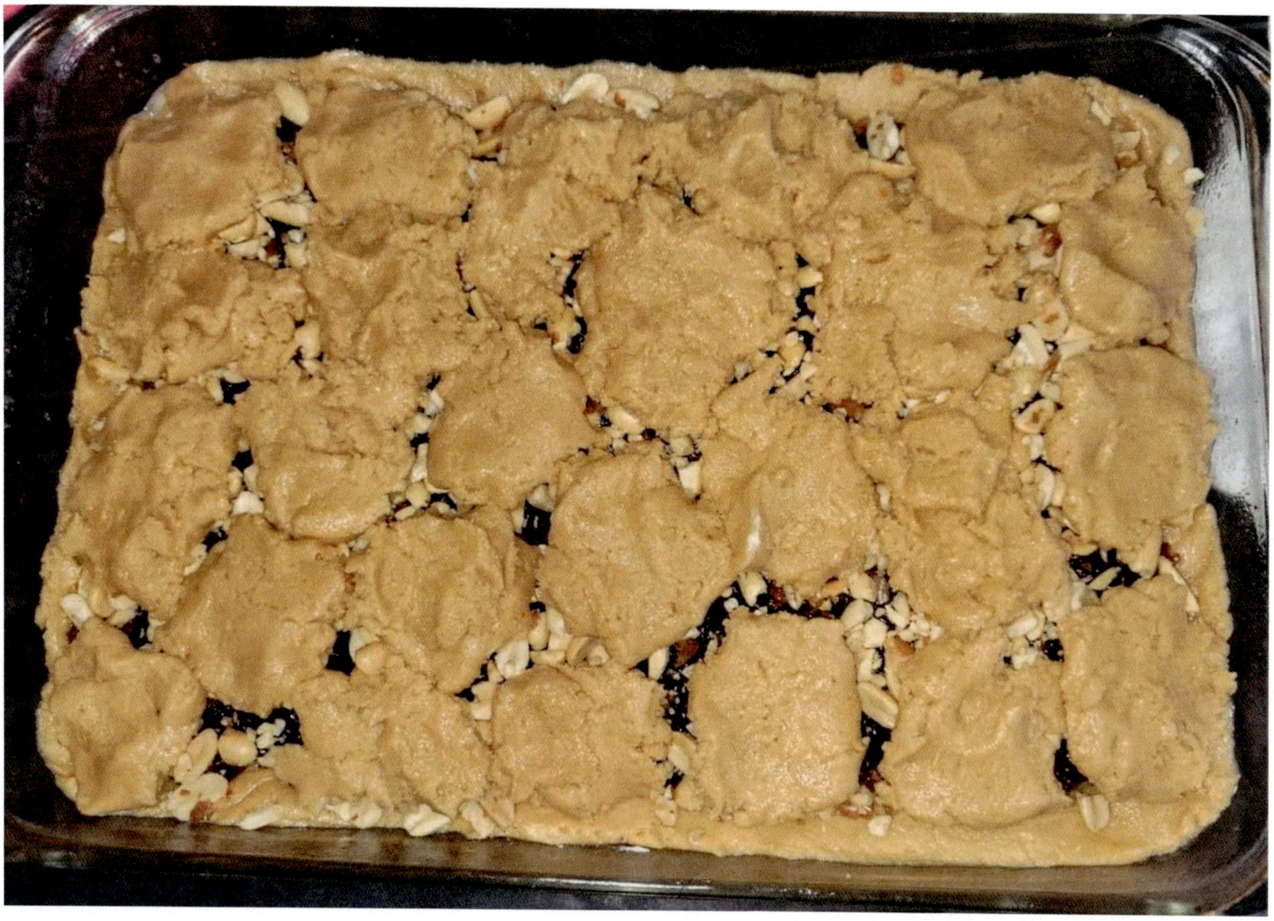

JAMMY BAR COOKIES

Ingredients:

1/2 lb Butter

1 Cup Sugar

2 Egg yolks

2 Cups Flour

3/4 Cup Strawberry jam (I like guava jam)

1 1/4 Cup Chopped walnuts

Directions:

Preheat oven to 325 degrees. Grease an 8" square baking pan. In a mixing bowl, cream the butter until soft. Gradually add the sugar, creaming till light and fluffy. Add the egg yolks and blend well. Spoon half the batter into the cake pan and spread it evenly pressing into corners. Top with the jam, but be careful not to let it touch the sides of the pan, or it will stick. Then, with the remaining dough, I smash a Tbsp size in the palm of my hands and, lay it down & pat it gently & place it like a puzzle on top of the jam. It's ok if some jam shows between pieces it does not have to be perfectly flat. Bake for 1 hour, let cool and cut into 1 x 2 inch bars. You can use any type of jam if you prefer and get creative.

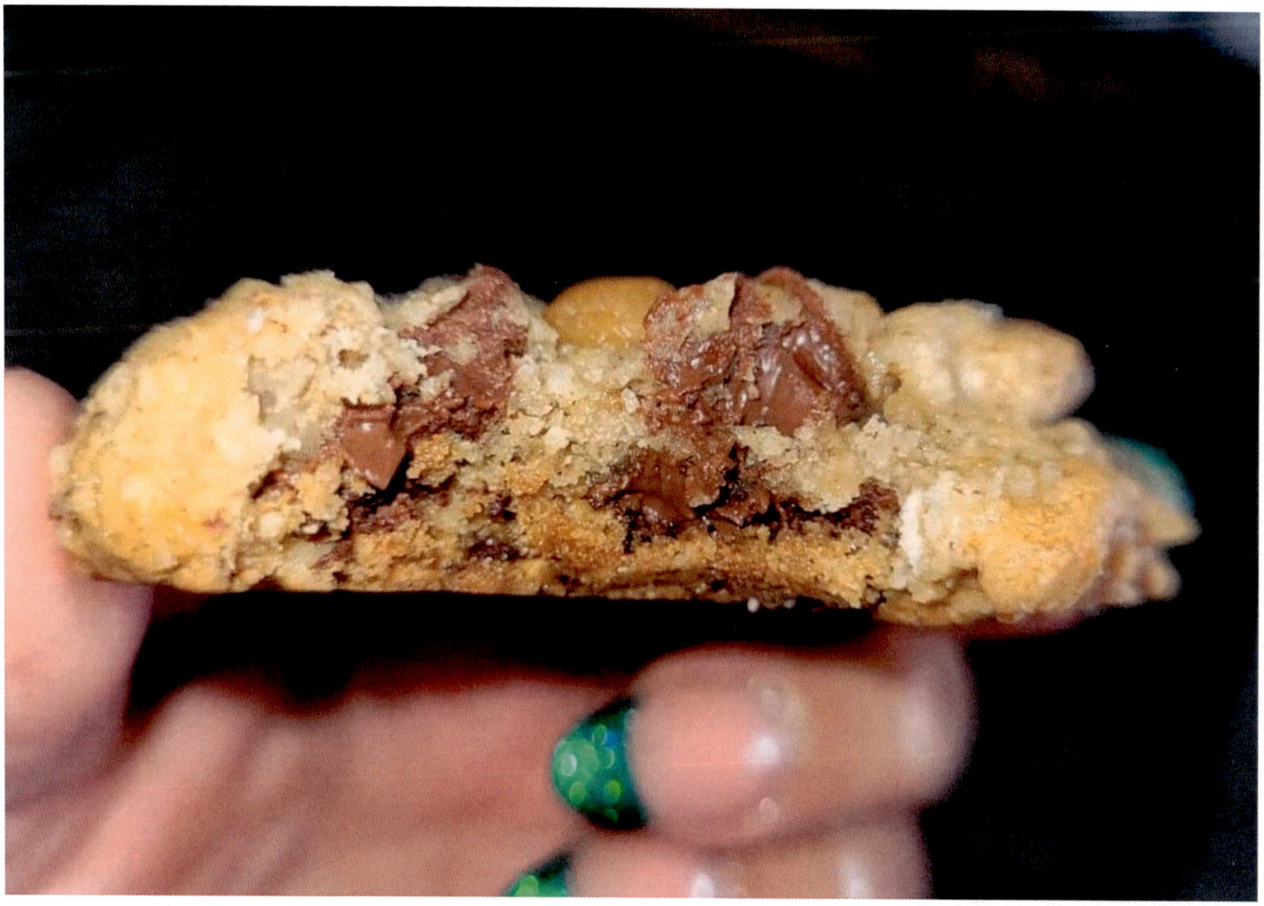

DECADENT CHOCOLATE CHIP COOKIES

Ingredients:

1/2 Cup rolled oats

1-1/2 Cup flour

2-1/4 tsp. Baking soda

1 tsp. Salt

1/2 tsp. Cinnamon

3 Cups Semi-sweet chocolate chips

1-1/2 Cups finely chopped pecans toasted

1 Cup Butter softened

3/4 Cup packed brown sugar

2 tsp. Vanilla

1/2 tsp. Lemon juice

2 Eggs

Directions:

1. Grind oats in a food processor or blender until fine. Combine the oats with the flour, baking soda, salt & cinnamon in a medium bowl.
2. Cream together the butter, sugars, vanilla and lemon juice in another medium bowl with an electric mixer. Add the eggs and mix till smooth. Stir in the dry mix into the wet mixture and blend well. Add the chocolate chips and nuts to the dough and mix until the ingredients are well blended.
3. For best results, chill the dough in the refrigerator before baking the cookies for about 4 hours or longer.
4. Spoon rounded portions onto an ungreased cookie sheet. Place them 2 inches apart. Bake in a 350-degree oven for 12-15 minutes or light brown and soft in the middle. Cool and store in a sealed container. These taste like the cookies you get at check-in at the Double Tree Hotel.

COOKING WITH GANAS & ALOHA

THE BEST OATMEAL CHOCOLATE CHIP COOKIES

Ingredients:

1 Cup Shortening

1 Cup Granulated sugar

1 Cup Firmly packed brown sugar

2 Eggs

2 Tbsp Milk

1 1/2 tsp. Vanilla extract

1 1/2 Cups Flour

1/2 tsp. Salt

1 tsp. Baking soda

4 Cups Old-fashioned oats

1 1/2 cups semi-sweet chocolate chips

Directions:

Heat the Oven to 375. In a large bowl, blend the shortening and sugar cream together. Add eggs, milk and vanilla. Beat well. Add flour, salt, and soda. Beat well. Stir in oats and chocolate chips. Drop by rounded tablespoon fulls 2 inches apart onto an ungreased cookie sheet. Bake for 15 min or till golden brown. Remove from oven, let stand for 10 min and cool on a wire rack till completely cooled. Yields 40 cookies.

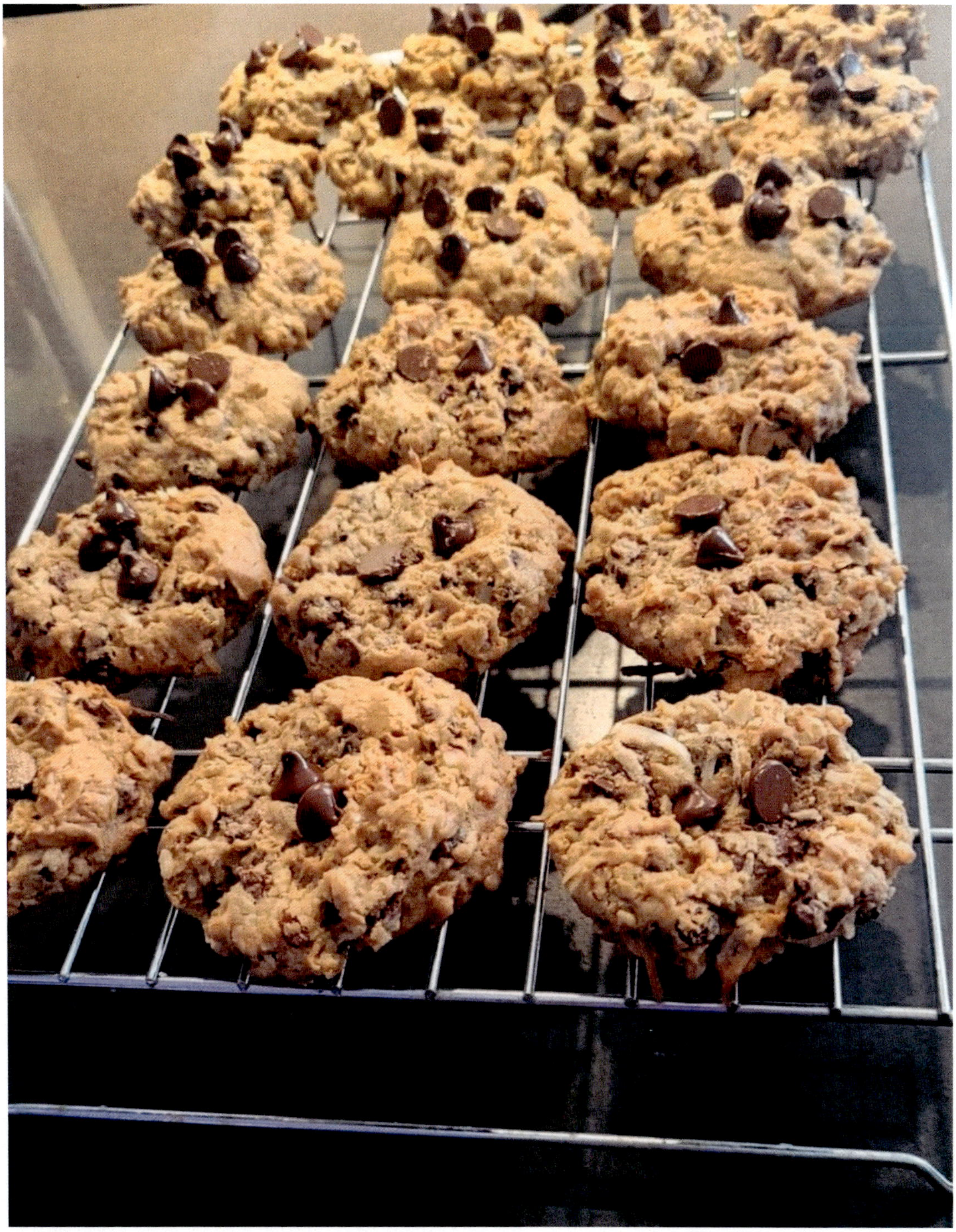

COOKING WITH GANAS & ALOHA

FUN FUSION COOKIES

Ingredients:

1 Cup Unsalted butter melted till browned

1 1/2 Cups Light Brown sugar packed

1/2 Cup Granulated sugar

2 Large eggs

1 Large egg yolk

2 tsp Vanilla extract

2 1/3 Cups all-purpose flour

1 tsp Baking soda

2 tsp ground cinnamon

1 tsp Kosher salt (you can use sea salt)

2 Cups Old-fashioned oats

1/2 cup Shredded coconut

1/2 Cup Pecans chopped

1/2 Cup Walnuts chopped

1 1/2 Cups semi-sweet chocolate chips

1 Cup Mini chocolate chips

1/2 Cup raisins

Instructions:

Preheat oven to 350 degrees. Line Cookie sheets with parchment paper. In a large bowl, beat together the butter and both sugars until well combined. Add the eggs and yolk, beating until well combined. Add the vanilla. Now, add the flour, baking soda, cinnamon, & salt and mix well. Add the Oats, coconut, chocolate chips, pecans, walnuts & raisins. Scoop about 2-inch balls of dough onto the lined baking sheets, leaving about 2" in between each ball. Bake 12-15 minutes until the cookies are golden brown and still slightly soft in the center. Cool on a wire rack. Yields about 3 dozen cookies.

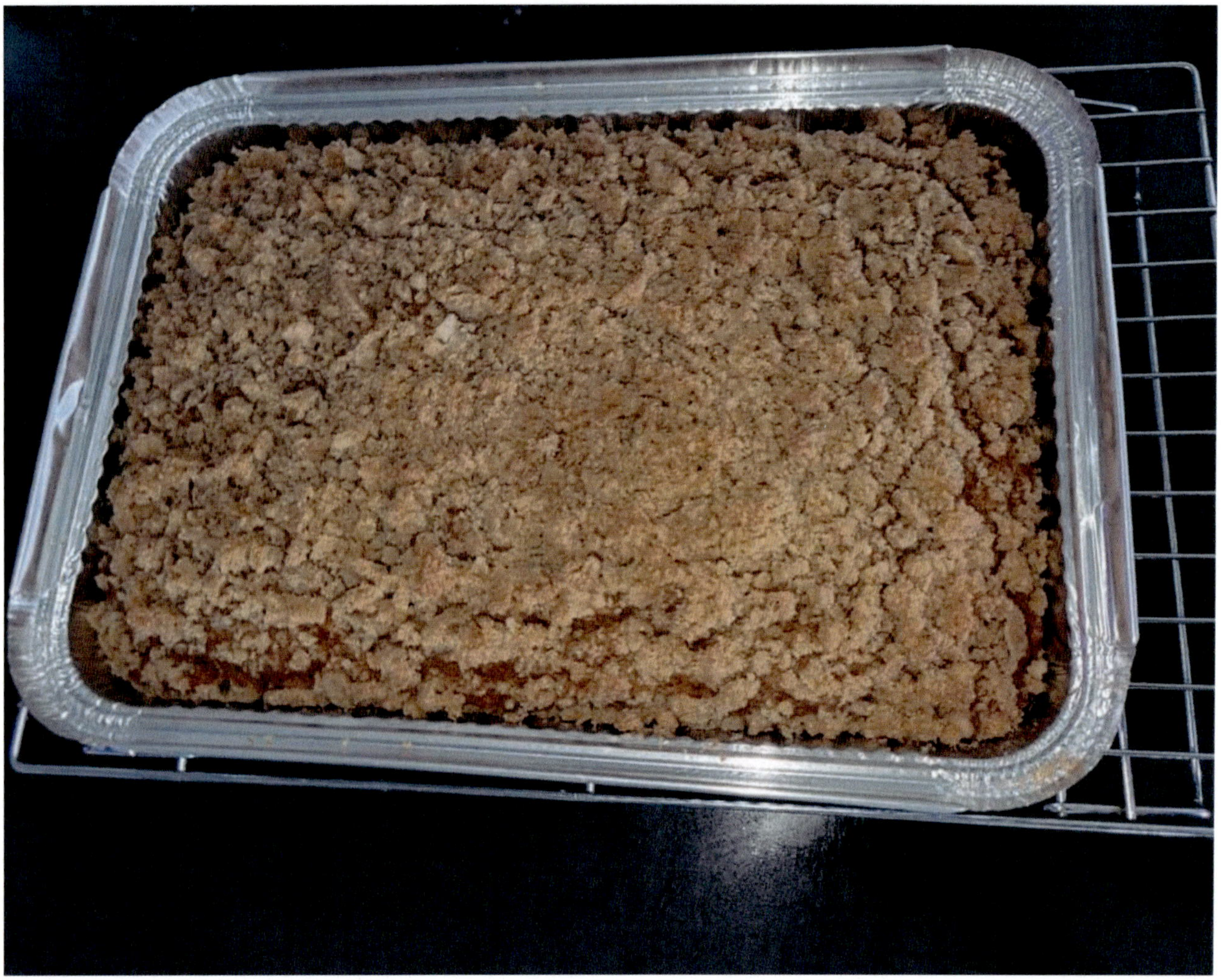

CAFETERIA COFFEE CAKE

Ingredients:

2 1/2 Cups flour

1 Cup brown sugar

3/4 tsp cinnamon

1 tsp baking powder

1 Cup buttermilk

1 tsp baking soda

1 Egg

3/4 Cup oil

Directions:

Mix dry ingredients, add liquids, and mix lightly.

Bake in a prepared pan at 350 degrees for about 45 minutes.

These recipes provide a variety of flavors and textures, perfect for any baking enthusiast looking to expand their dessert repertoire.

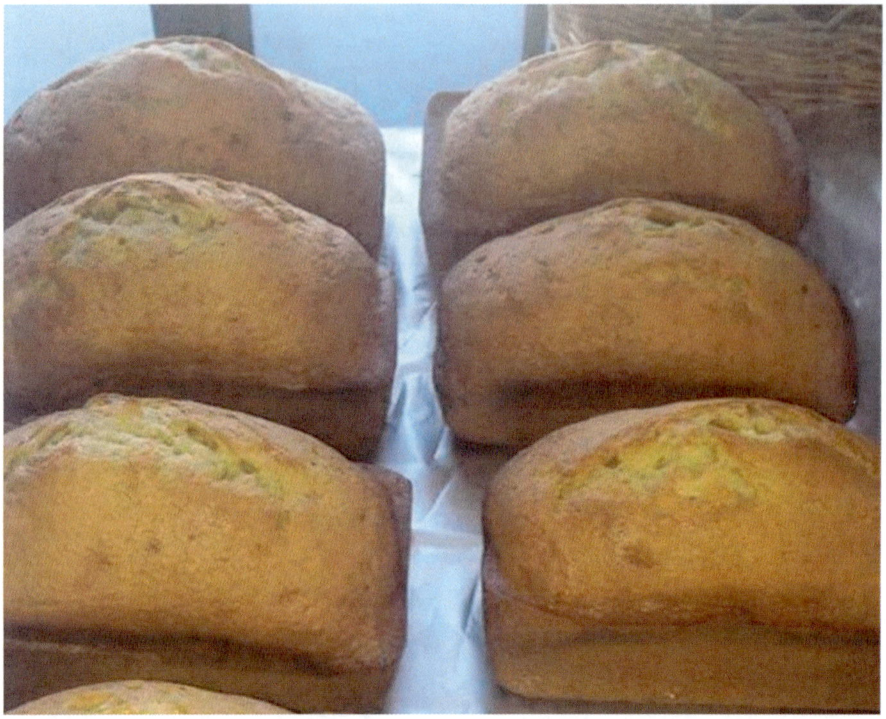

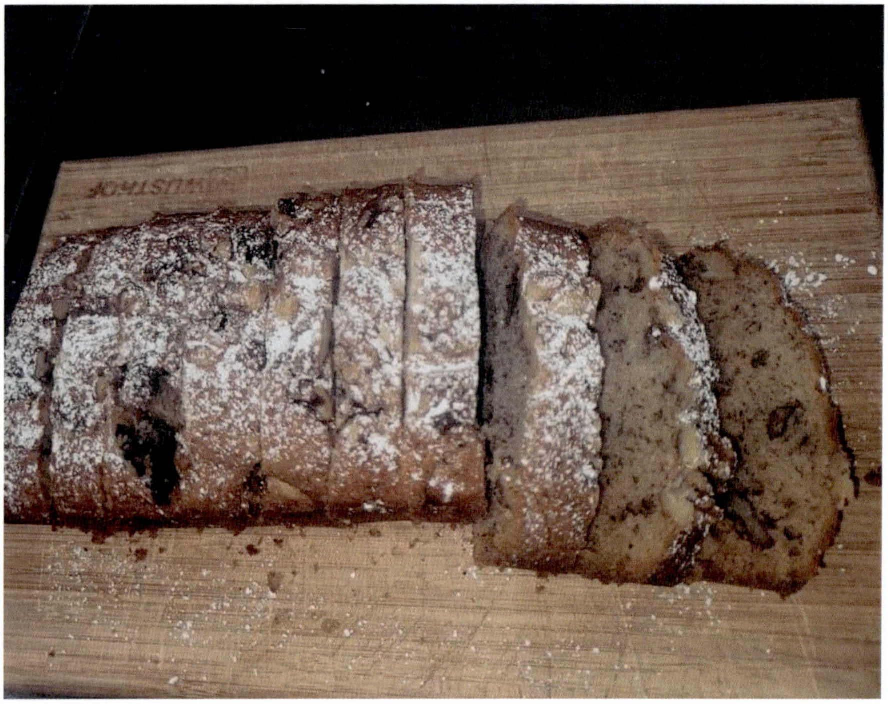

COOKING WITH GANAS & ALOHA

MY BANANA BREAD

Ingredients:

1 Cup Sugar

1/2 Cup Margarine

2 Eggs

3 Mashed ripe bananas

2 Cups Flour

1/2 Cup chopped nuts

1/2 Tsp Salt

1 Tsp Soda

Directions:

Beat margarine and sugar till creamy; add the 2 eggs and mix well; add the flour, salt, and soda and mix well.

Add flour, and beat well so the mixture will be thick; add the mashed bananas, it will be creamy; fold in nuts.

Place in well well-sprayed loaf pan with cooking spray.

Bake at 350 degrees for about 45 min.

Yields 3 to 4 mini loaf pans or 2 full medium-size loaf pans (Fill 3/4 way it rises high).

Let it cool for 10 min and remove from pans. Cool on a wire rack before slicing.

I put a little powdered sugar in a small sieve and tap the sides over the bread for a little added sweetness and décor.

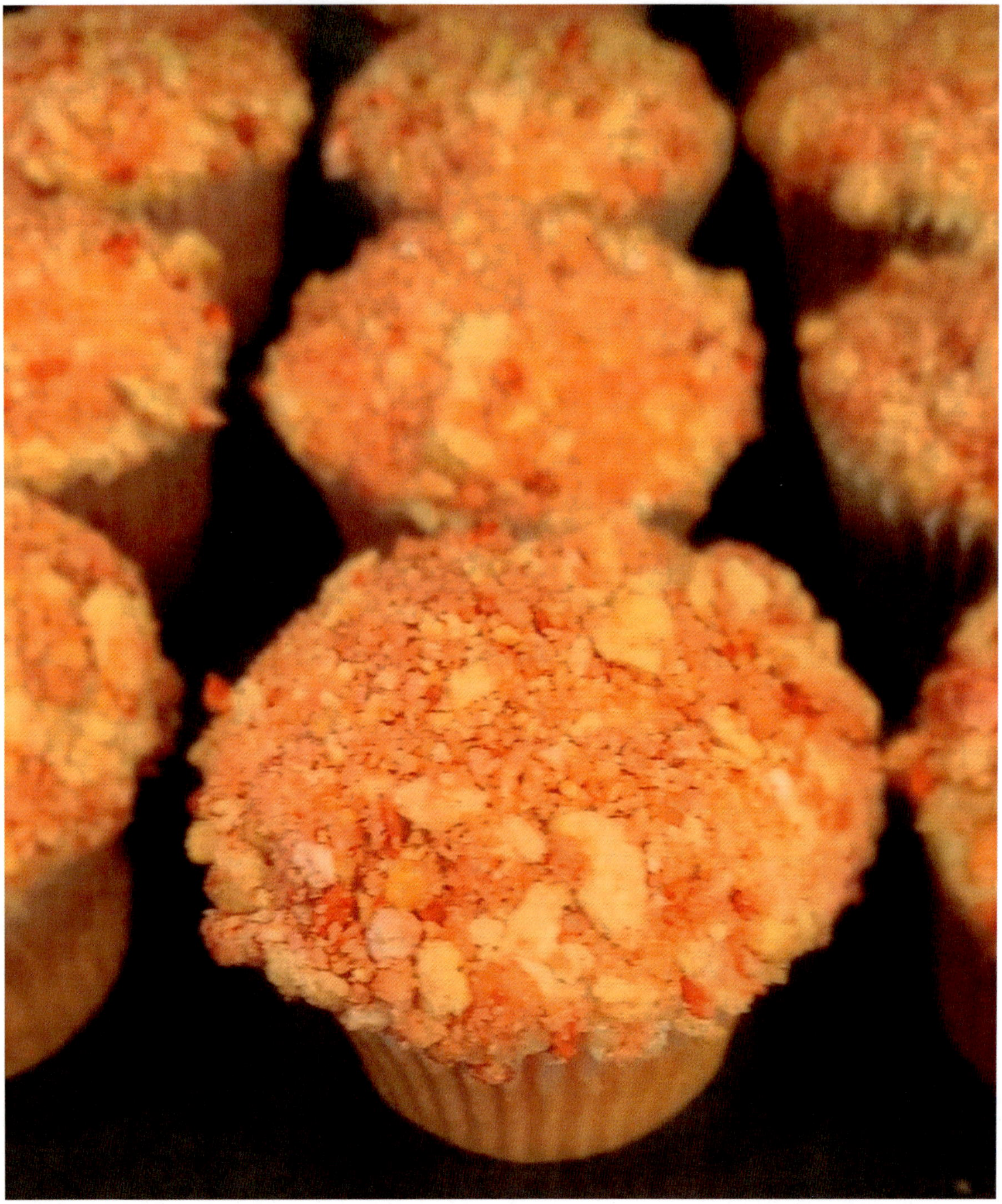

STRAWBERRY SHORTCAKE MUFFINS

Ingredients:

2 Cups all-purpose flour

1 1/2 tsp baking powder

1/2 tsp salt

1 Cup whole milk

1/4 Cup butter, melted

1 Egg

1/2 tsp strawberry extract

OR

1 box of Strawberry cake mix and follow directions.

1/4 Cup strawberry jam

24 cupcake liners

Buttercream Frosting:

1 block of cream cheese

1 cup butter

1 1/2 cups confectioners' sugar

Strawberry Shortcake Topping:

2 cups freeze-dried strawberries

20 golden oreos

1/4 cup melted butter

Directions:

Preheat oven to 350 degrees, line muffin pans with liners.
In a large bowl, whisk flour, baking powder, and salt.
In a separate bowl, mix melted butter, milk, egg, and strawberry extract.
Gradually blend wet ingredients into dry; do not overmix.
Spoon half the batter into liners, add a dollop of jam, then top with the remaining batter.
Bake for about 15-20 minutes. Cool and top with buttercream.

Next:
 Put the Strawberries and Oreos into a food processor and pulse till it forms small pebbles. Place on a cookie sheet spread out and drizzle the melted butter over the crumbles.

Take the frosted cupcake and carefully scoop the strawberry Oreo crumbs on top and all around the buttercream.

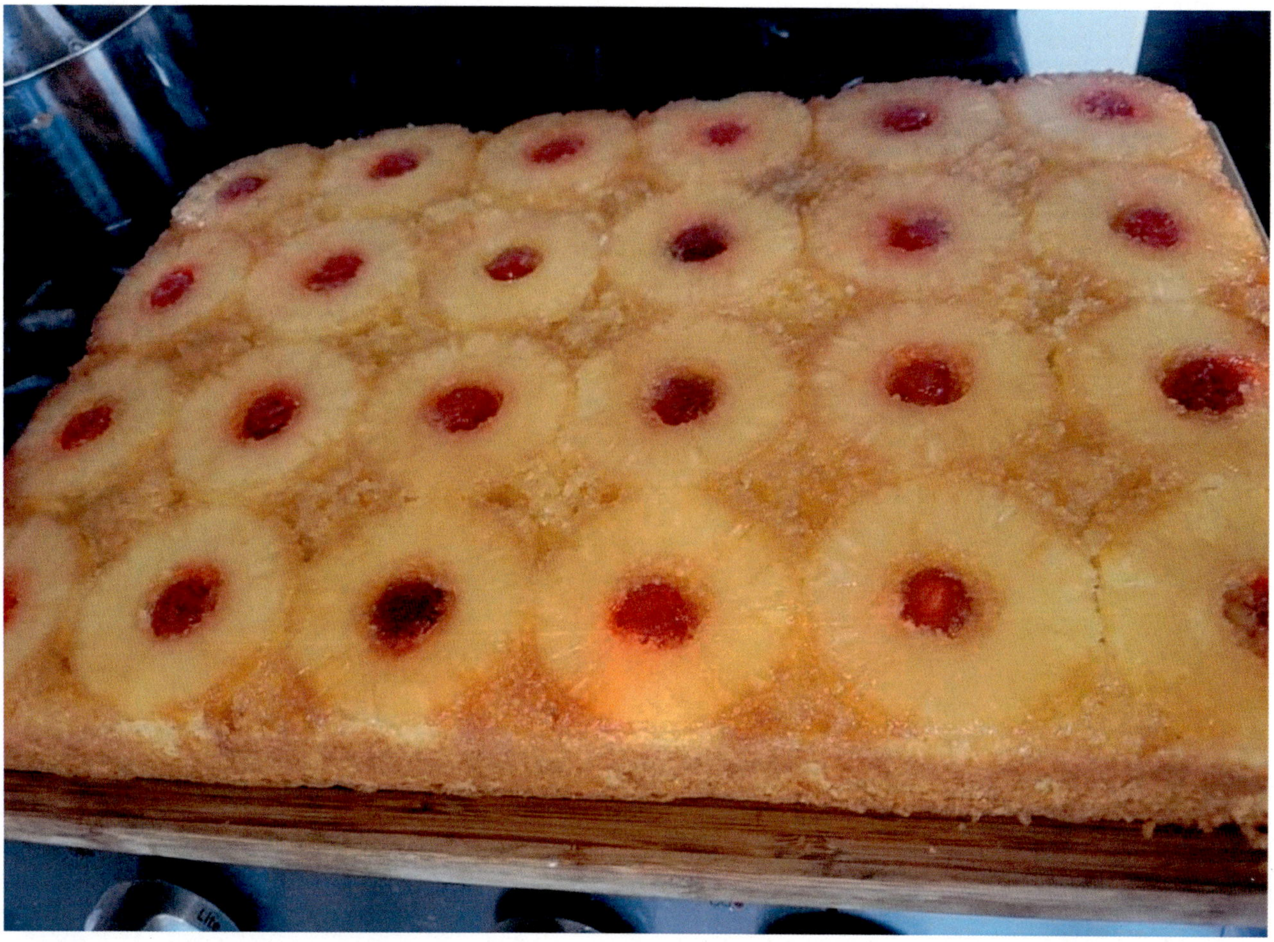

PINEAPPLE UPSIDE DOWN CAKE

Ingredients:

*(For a 13x9 cake pan) (For ½ sheet 3 boxes triple recipe)

1 Box of pineapple supreme cake mix OR I use yellow cake mix you will need oil & 3 eggs for cake box recipe.

1 Cup Brown sugar

1 Can pineapple rings.

½ Stick melted butter or margarine

Maraschino cherries (no stems)

Walnuts or macadamia nuts optional

Directions:

Follow the directions on the cake mix but instead of the 1 cup of water you will drain the juice from the can pineapple. Make sure you push the top of the can down on the pineapple rings hard because it equal exactly 1 Cup of pineapple juice. Follow the rest of the recipe exactly. Place bowl of cake batter aside.

Now take your 13x9 inch cake pan and spray the side only with baking spray to prevent sticking. Melt the butter in a sauce pan and pour it into the bottom of the cake pan making sure its evenly coated on bottom. Sprinkle your brown sugar evenly on top of the butter.

Now place your pineapple rings where you want them and place a cherry in the center of the ring. You can place your nuts in between the spaces of rings. Carefully pour batter over the rings being careful not to disturb the bottom. Use a rubber spatula to evenly spread the top. Bake 1 hour 350 degrees cool 5 min. run a butter knife around ends & take your cake board place on the top of pan holding the pan firmly gently and turn over quickly and gently tap the bottom of the pan. If any rings get stuck to pan use a metal spatula and gently flip back on cake Cool on a wire rack. Cut and enjoy.

COOKING WITH GANAS & ALOHA

CARROT CAKE

Ingredients:

2 Cups flour

2 Cups sugar

2 tsp baking powder

1 tsp baking soda

1 tsp salt

1 Tbsp cinnamon

1 Cup oil

4 Eggs

2 Cups shredded carrots

2 Cups walnuts (optional)

Cream Cheese Frosting:

1 8 oz block cream cheese

1 cube butter

Powdered sugar to taste

Directions:

Mix dry ingredients, add oil and eggs, and mix till combined.

Stir in carrots and nuts.

Bake in a prepared pan at 350 degrees for about 60 minutes.

Cool and frost with cream cheese frosting.

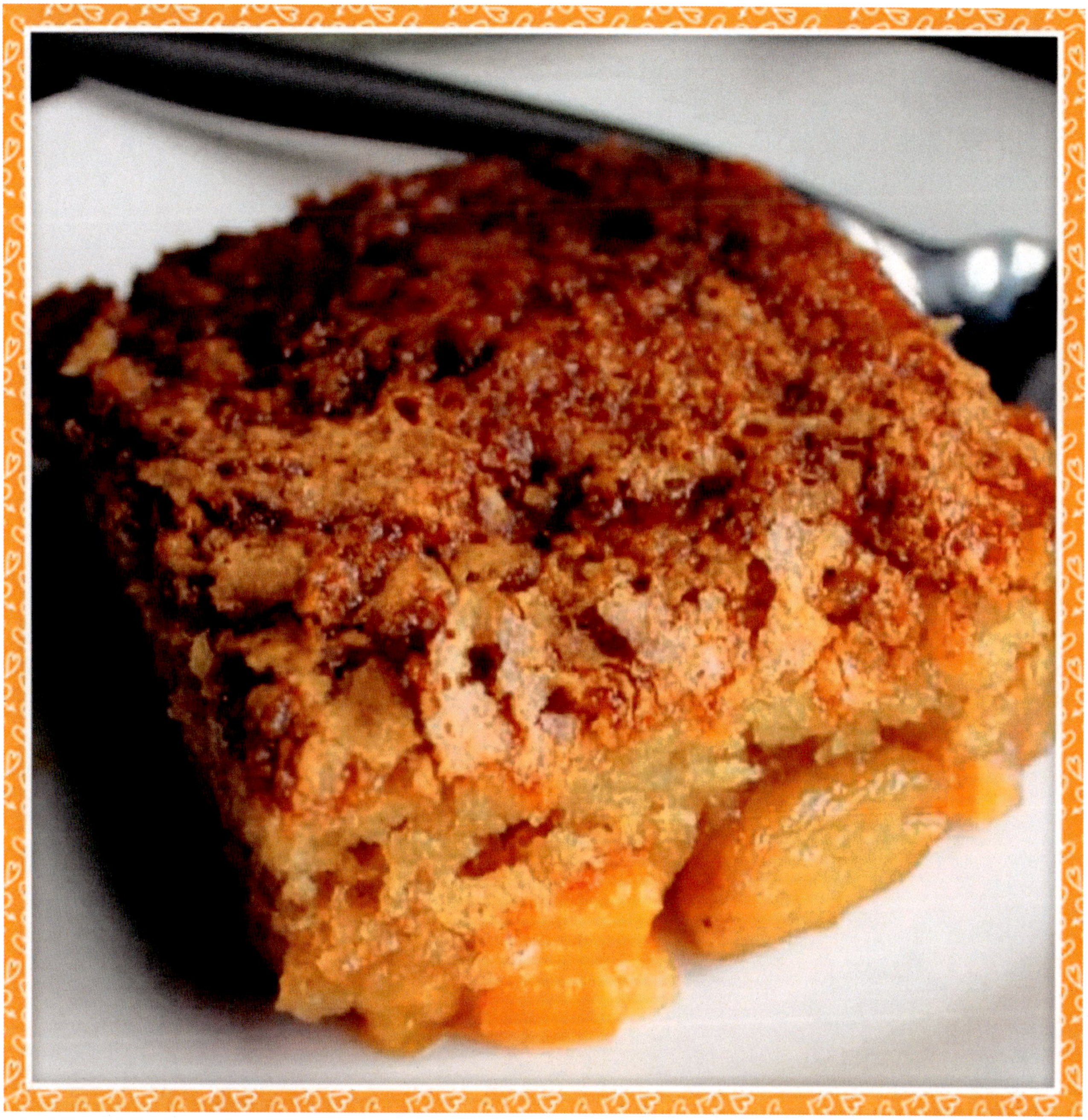

TEACHERS CAKE

Ingredients:

2 Cups flour

2 Eggs

2 tsp baking soda

1 15 oz can fruit cocktailsss

Topping:

1/2 Cup brown sugar

1/2 Cup chopped walnuts

Sauce:

3/4 Cup butter

3/4 Cup evaporated milk

Directions:

Mix all ingredients and bake in a greased pan at 350 degrees for about 30 minutes.

Combine topping ingredients and add to the cake.

Boil butter and milk, and pour over the hot cake.

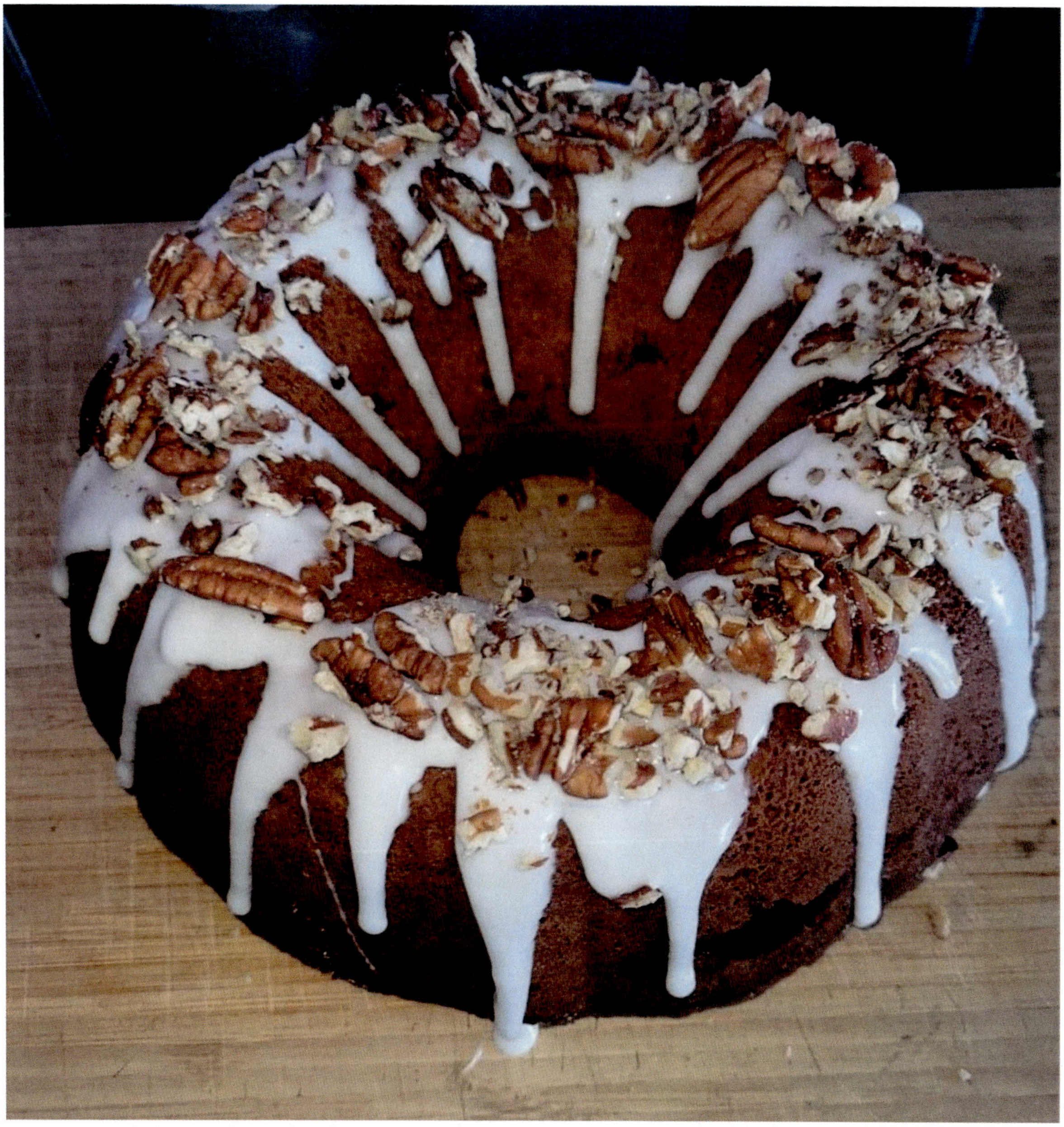

SOCK IT TO ME CAKE

Ingredients:

1 Package yellow cake mix

1 Cup sour cream

1/2 Cup oil

1/4 Cup sugar

1 Cup pecans

2 Tbsp brown sugar

2 Tbsp cinnamon

Glaze:

1 Cup powdered sugar

2 Tbsp milk

Directions:

Mix cake ingredients and pour into a greased bundt pan.

Combine pecans, brown sugar, and cinnamon, and add to batter.

Bake, cool, and drizzle with glaze.

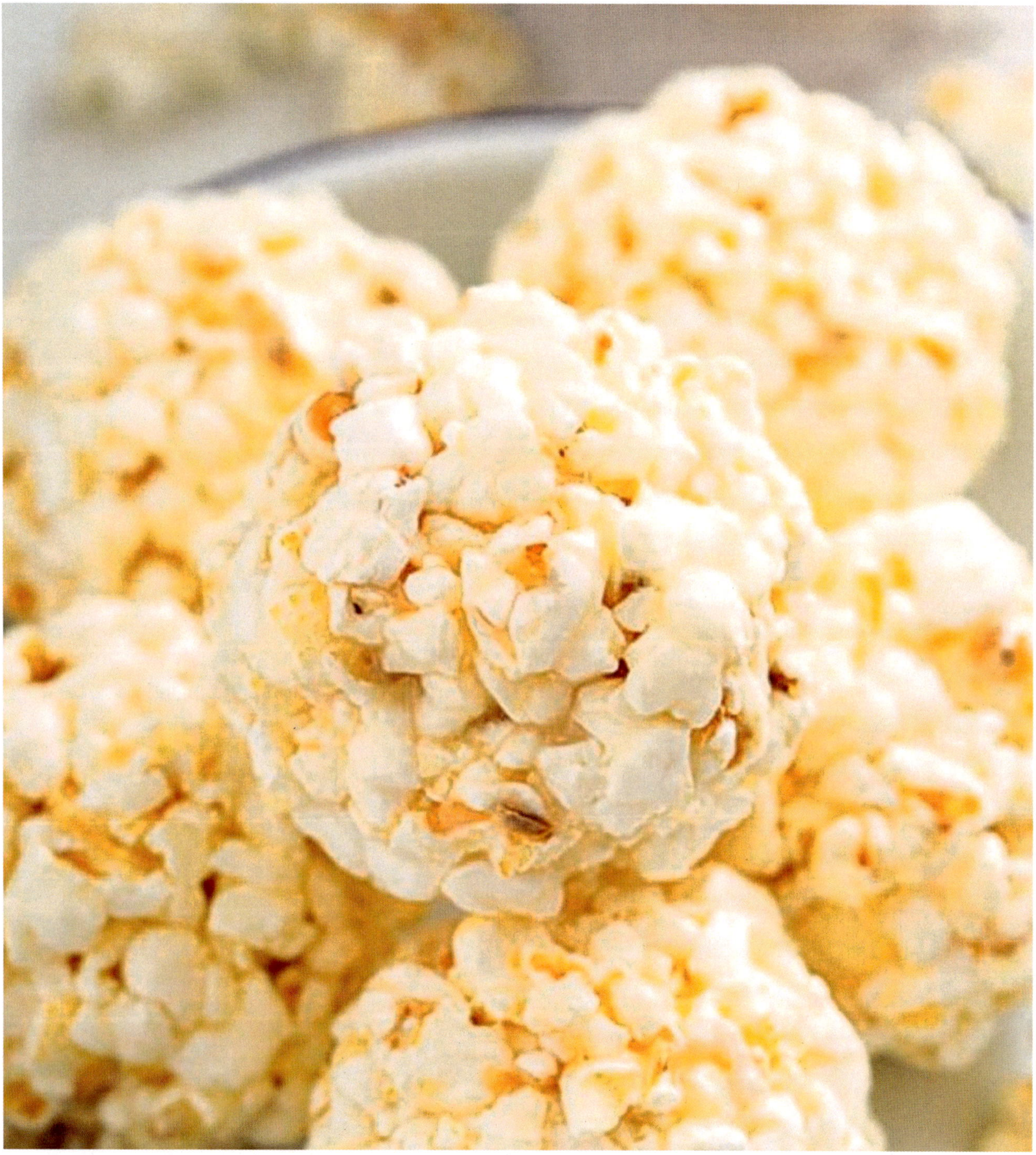

POPCORN BALLS

Ingredients:

2 Cups White sugar

1 1/2 Cups Water

1/2 Cup Light corn syrup

1 tsp. Vanilla extract

5 quarts of Popped popcorn

1 tsp. Distilled white vinegar

1/2 tsp. Salt

Directions:

1. Butter the sides of a large saucepan. In the saucepan, combine the sugar, water, salt, corn syrup and vinegar. Cook over medium heat to the hard ball stage of a candy thermometer to 250 degrees F (120 degrees C). Stir in the vanilla and slowly pour the hot mixture over the popped popcorn, stirring to mix well.
2. Butter your hands lightly and shape into balls pressing tightly. BE CAREFUL mixture will be HOT. Place balls onto waxed paper and cool to room temp. Seal in cello bags and tie off with a cute ribbon.

If you want your popcorn balls to have color to match a theme add food coloring to your hot mixture before pouring over the popcorn.

COOKING WITH GANAS & ALOHA

PEANUT BRITTLE

Ingredients:

1 Cup Granulated sugar

1/2 Cup Light corn syrup

1/4 Cup Water

1 Cup Peanuts (no skins)

2 Tbsp Softened butter

1 Tsp Baking soda

Directions:

Grease a cookie sheet (I use cooking spray). Set aside In a heavy 2-quart saucepan over med. Heat bring the sugar, corn syrup, salt, and water to a boil. Stir till sugar is dissolved. Set the candy thermometer in place and continue cooking. Stir frequently till the temp reaches 300 degrees or until a small amount of the mix is dropped into very cold water and separated into hard, brittle threads. Stir in peanuts and stir for another 2 minutes. Remove from heat and immediately stir in the butter and baking soda; pour all at once onto the baking sheet. I use a buttered rubber spatula to spread the mixture evenly. Let it cool completely till hard. I tap mine with a rolling pin to break it into nice-sized pieces.

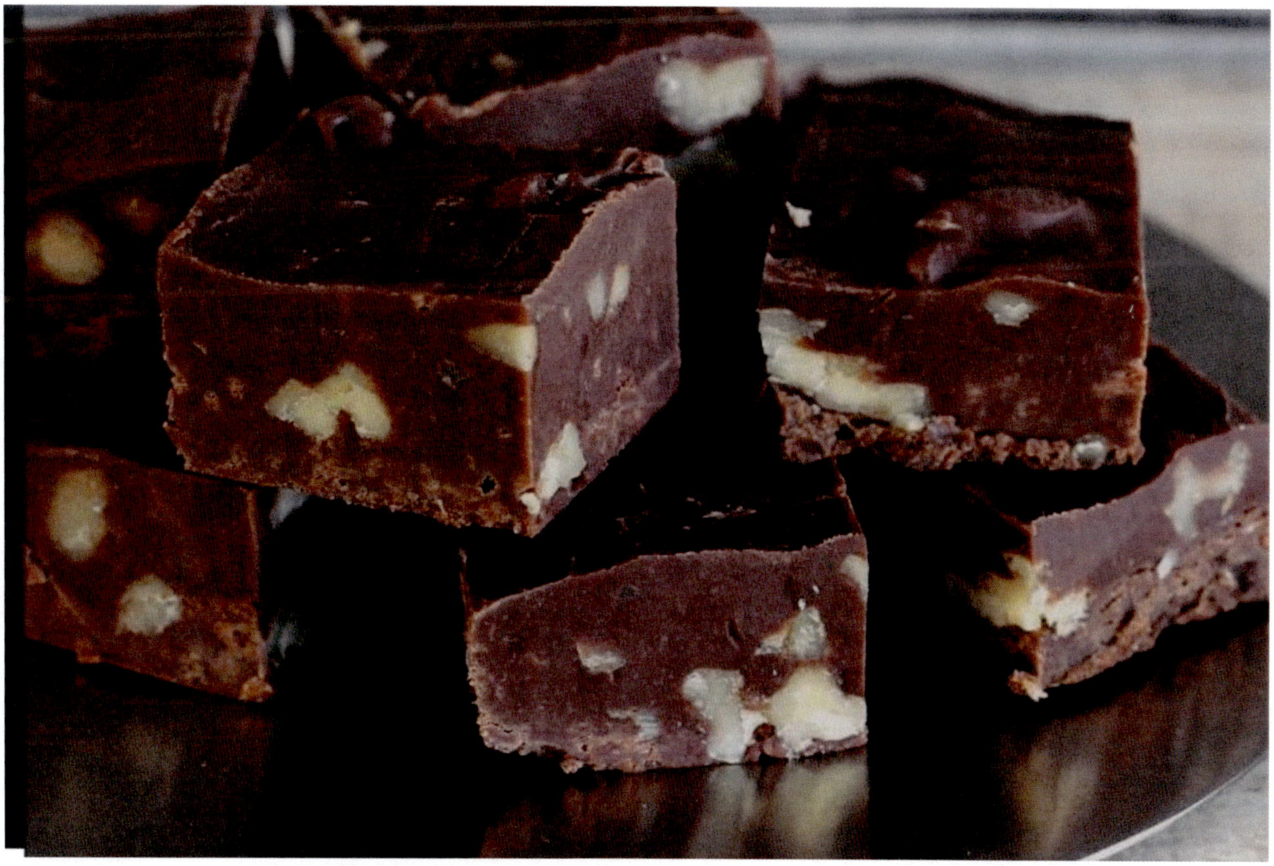

OLD FASHIONED FUDGE

Ingredients:

1 Cup Granulated sugar

3/4 Cup butter (1 1/2 sticks butter)

1 Sm. 5 oz Can evaporated milk (2/3 cup)

1 1/2 Pkg Semi-sweet chocolate chips

1 7 oz Jar marshmallow crème

1 Tsp Vanilla

1 Cup Walnuts (I like pecans)

Directions:

In a heavy saucepan, bring the milk, sugar, and butter to a boil, stirring constantly. Bring the boil till the candy thermometer reaches 234 degrees (About 4 to 5 min). After boiling, remove from heat. Stir in the chocolate chips and marshmallow crème till melted. Stir in the vanilla and walnuts. Spread into a waxed paper or foil-lined 9" square pan. Cool @ room temp about 4 hours. Lift the paper/foil out of the pan and cut into 1X1 inch squares. Yields: 3 lbs fudge

COOKING WITH GANAS & ALOHA

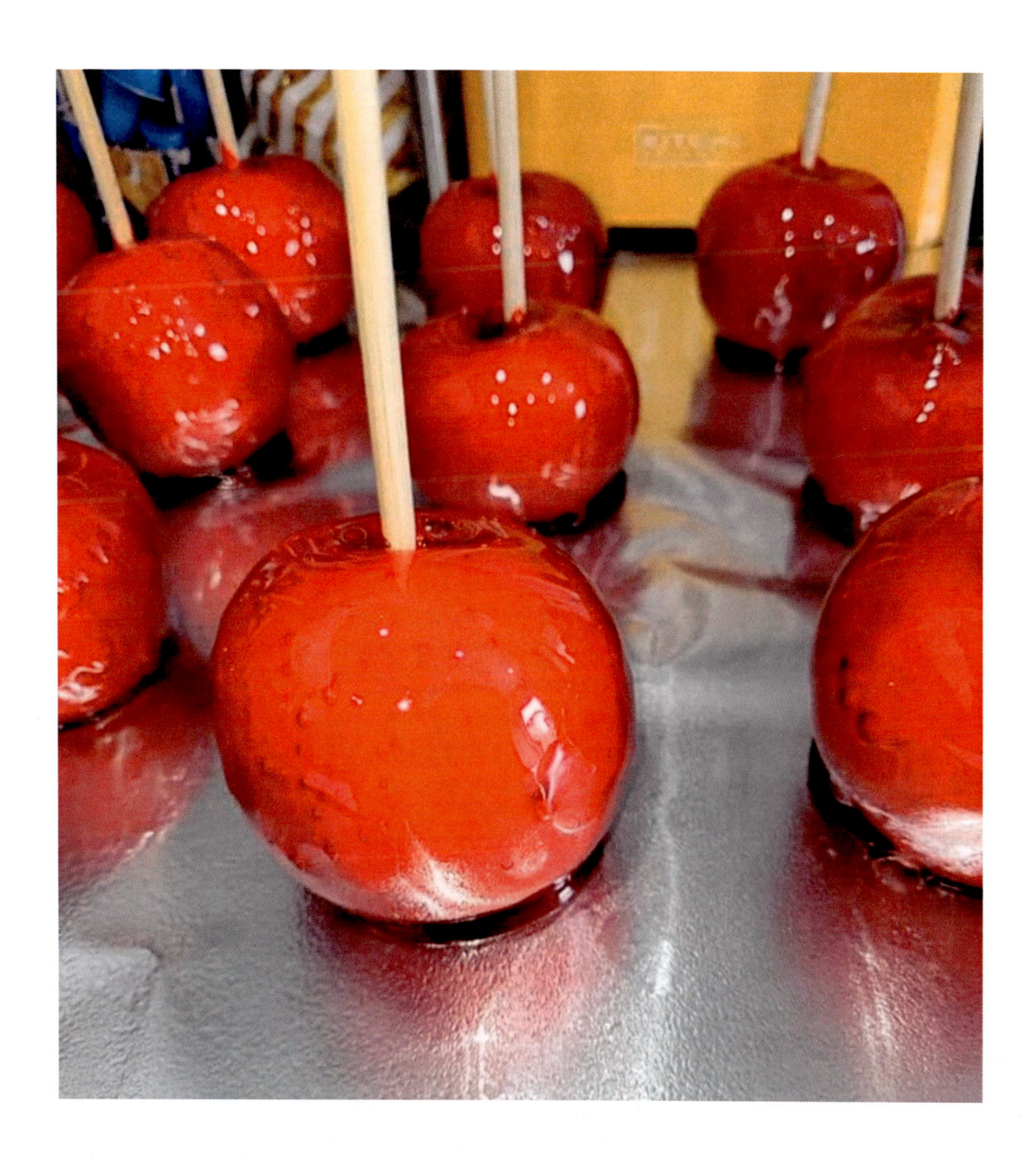

CINNAMON RED CANDY APPLES

Ingredients:

2 Cups Granulated sugar

1 Cup Light Corn syrup (If doubling recipe 1-16oz bottle = 2 C)

1/2 Cup water

6 Drops Cinnamon oil

15 Drops of red food coloring

8 Medium size red apples

8 Lollipop sticks 4 1/2" long

Directions:

Wash and dry apples. Remove stems and insert the lollipop sticks. Line a cookie sheet with foil and lightly butter the foil. Combine the sugar, corn syrup and water in a 2-quart heavy saucepan and stir till crystals are completely dissolved. Wash down the sides of the pan with a pastry brush dipped in hot water. Put on a candy thermometer and cook without stirring till it reaches 285 degrees. Remove from heat and stir in food coloring and cinnamon oil. Be careful to avoid inhaling the fumes from cinnamon. Tilt the pan slightly and, dip the apples and twirl till evenly coated and let excess drip off and place on cookie sheet til hardens. If storing, make sure you cover them with plastic and twist tie because they will attract moisture and become sticky. Any excess candy pour onto a buttered cookie sheet let cool and break with pastry roller into bite size pieces. Called Red glass.

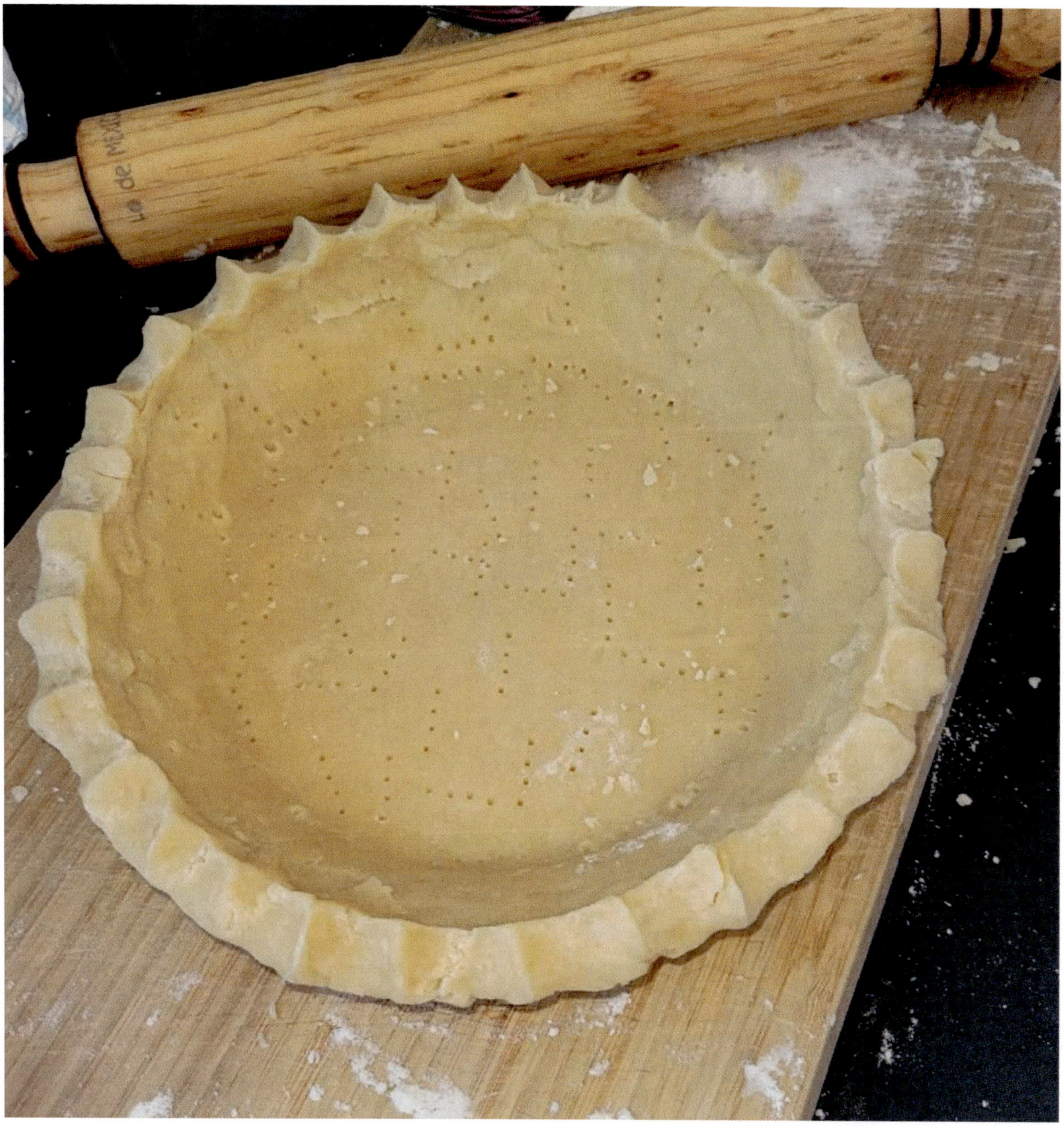

PIE CRUST (NO FAIL)

Ingredients:

1 Cup All purpose flour

1/3 Cup Shortening + 1 Tbsp

1/2 Tsp Salt

3 TBSP Cold water

Directions:

Place the flour and salt in a bowl and mix with your fingers till well mixed. Add the shortening and mix it into the flour till little pea size forms. NOW…CAREFULLY add the cold water and GENTLY mix with fingers till well incorporated. DO NOT knead this dough. Gently form it into a ball; it will be on the flaky side. Place on a lightly floured board and roll it out to fit bigger than your pie pan. Gently take your rolling pin and start to roll the dough around the pin lightly and, place the pin over the pan and start unrolling. If the crust cracks, it's okay just press back in place into the pan. Take the ends and bring them over to the edges of the pan and form a nice rim, pinching between your fingers to form a pretty rim. Poke holes with a fork on the bottom and sides of the crust to reduce shrinkage and bubbling when baking or you can use pie weights. This is a really flaky crust. *The key is to not overwork the dough and not knead it.*

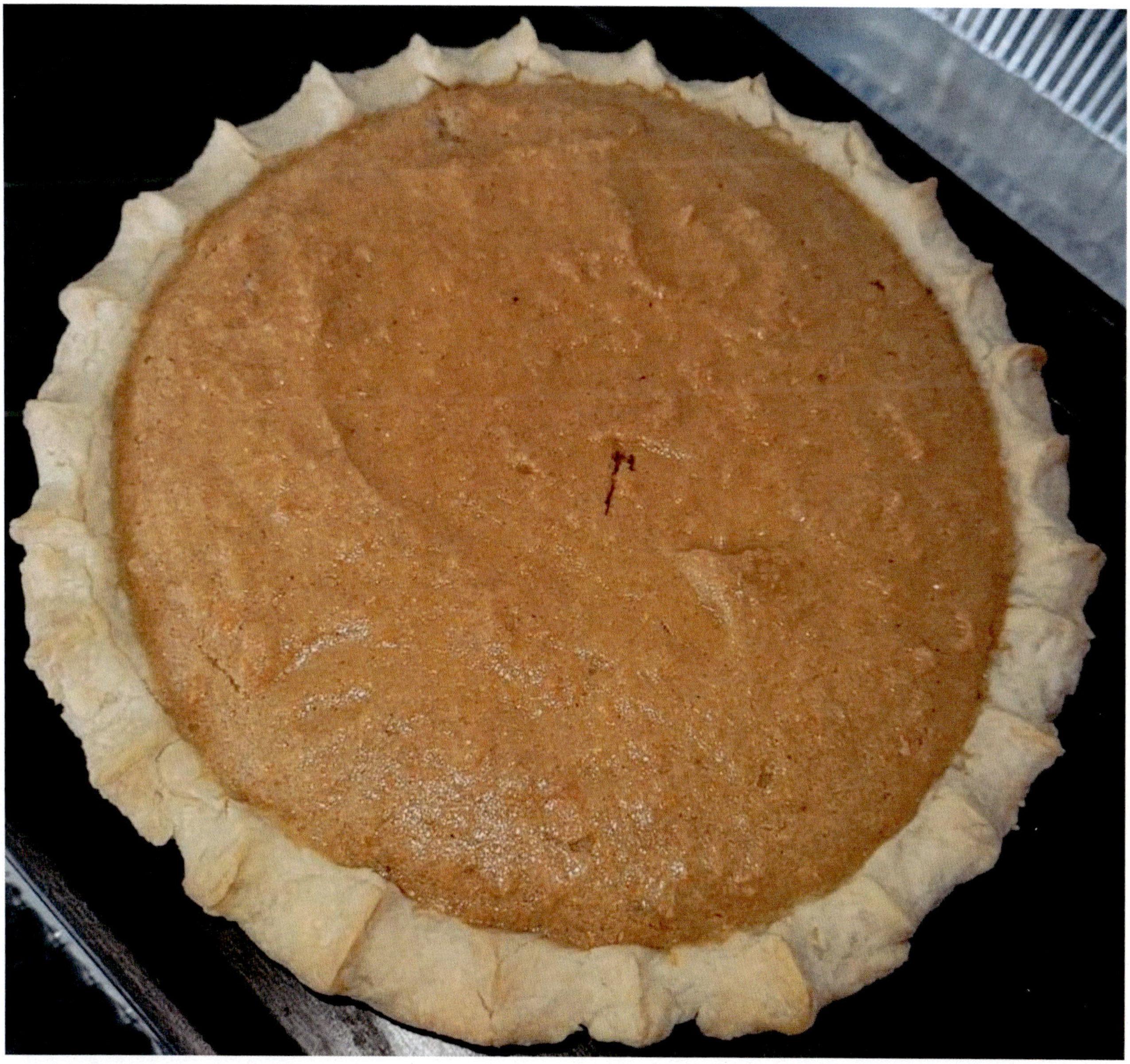

SOUTHERN SWEET POTATO PIE

Ingredients:

4 oz softened butter (1 stick)

2 Cups Cooked, peeled sweet potatoes mashed

2 Cups Granulated sugar

1 Small can (5 oz, about 1/2 Cup + 2 Tbsp) evaporated milk

1 Tsp. Vanilla

3 Eggs beaten

1 1/2 Tsp. Cinnamon

2 prepared 8-inch pie shells

Directions:

Mix butter, potatoes, sugar, evaporated milk until well blended. Add the vanilla, eggs and cinnamon, and mix well. Pour into the pie shells. Bake in a 350-degree oven for about 1 hour till the knife pierced in the center comes out clean. Cool. Garnish with whip cream.

Note: I use this recipe for a 9" pie; I fill it to the bottom of the line from the pie crust because when it cools, it will shrink down.

My pie crust is in this cookbook.

COOKING WITH GANAS & ALOHA

COOKING WITH GANAS & ALOHA

COOKING WITH GANAS & ALOHA

COOKING WITH GANAS & ALOHA

COOKING WITH GANAS & ALOHA

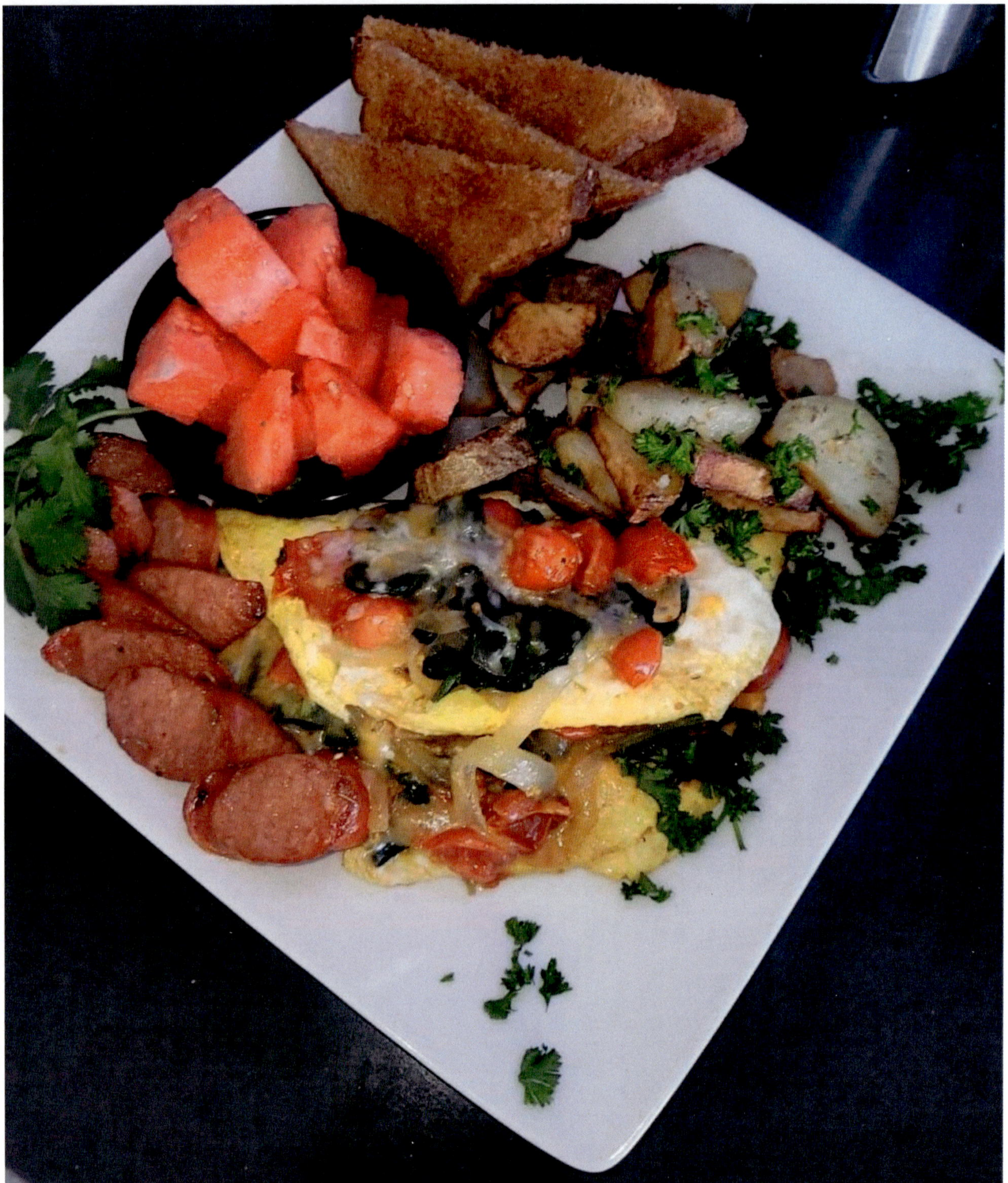

COOKING WITH GANAS & ALOHA

PLATING IDEAS

Plating is an indispensable aspect of cooking, as the visual presentation of your food can make a significant impact on the dining experience. This is particularly crucial for those who will be indulging in your culinary masterpieces. A well-plated dish can elevate the taste and aroma of the food, while a poorly presented dish can deter people from even trying it. Hence, it is vital to focus on plating and ensure that your dishes look appetizing and appealing. You find yourself uttering, 'Oh man, that looks incredible!' And when you take that first bite, the taste lives up to your expectations. The subsequent pages showcase plating ideas for dishes I have created and arranged. For me, a satisfying breakfast is crucial for my husband, as he is the king of our home and should be pampered accordingly. Making his meals visually appealing is my top priority.

When I humbly lay his plate before him at the table, whether for breakfast, lunch, or dinner, he is overjoyed. Remember, presentation and plating can draw attention to the specific ingredients in a dish, whether for aesthetic or practical reasons. It highlights creativity and culinary expertise. It elevates the look, taste, and overall experience of the meal, leaving a lasting impression on your patron.

It is of utmost importance to garnish your plates to make it appealing to the eye because after all it is said "We eat with our eyes first".

Made in the USA
Monee, IL
06 June 2024

2e21e62b-914e-4ce5-a0f8-1fbfaf97a476R01